DOCTOR ZHIVAGO
David Lean

**MARC
BRINCOURT
GUILLAUME
CLAVIÈRES**

Text by
**JEAN-PIERRE
BOUYXOU**

On Set and Off Guard

Behind the Scenes with the Movie Greats

Dr. **STRANGELOVE**
Stanley Kubrick
George C. scott

First published in the United Kingdom in 2002 by
Thames & Hudson Ltd,
181A High Holborn, London WC1V 7QX

Original title : *Stars en liberté, les plus belles photos de tournage*
by : Marc Brincourt et Guillaume Clavières
Texts by : Jean-Pierre Bouyxou
Published by Editions Filipacchi in 2002
© 2002 Filipacchi Publishing

British Library Cataloguing-in-Publication Data
A catalogue record for this book is available from the British Library

ISBN 0-500-51111-X

Printed in France

Contents

Introduction

These are not official pictures, arranged by press agents for promotional purposes. Nor are they posed portraits or film stills taken during shooting. They are candid shots, taken under the non-negotiated, non-negotiable conditions of reportage. Once there was a time when stars were so big that they weren't afraid to be seen at work, or to invite photographers behind the scenes and into their dressing rooms. Marilyn Monroe, Audrey Hepburn, Sophia Loren, Ingrid Bergman, Marlon Brando, James Dean, Humphrey Bogart, Steve McQueen, and great directors like Huston, Scorsese and Fellini—they all knew and accepted that, in return for their status and international fame, the public would be allowed a glimpse behind the studio doors, and that in order to keep believing in them, loving them and applauding them, common mortals had to be able to reach out and touch the reality of their work. These photos are, and always will be, part of the glory and magic of filmmaking.

There is a natural connection between the fixed images of a still camera and the moving pictures of the cinema. Would Marilyn be Marilyn without all of those remarkable, beautiful photographs taken on film sets? These are the iconic images that are published in magazines, appear in endless books and hang on the walls in exhibitions. This is the stuff that movie legends are made of: Orson Welles, a huge sleeping Falstaff lying on a tabletop; Alfred Hitchcock or Federico Fellini acting out a scene for their stars; Bardot and Vadim hand in hand on the set of *And God... Created Woman*; Ava Gardner as *The Barefoot Contessa* with her feet in a bucket; Peter O'Toole, worn out by the role of *Lawrence of Arabia*; Marlene Dietrich reading a magazine between takes on *Judgment at Nuremberg*; and so many more.

Both intimate and professional, these pictures belong to movie mythology. Beyond their beauty, the talent of the photographers who took them and the stars who let them be taken, it is their authenticity that makes them a part of history, their total refusal to censure or flatter. These images are not simply nostalgic. They are cinema's past. And if the actors play their parts, they can still be its future.

Time Is on Our Side

or Between Takes

EXODUS
Otto Preminger
1960
Paul Newman
Paul Newman
mentally prepares
for his next scene.
Fascinated by
Leon Uris's novel,
Newman always
dreamed of
playing Ari Ben
Canaan, the young
officer who
brought several
hundred Jewish
refugees to Israel
in 1947 aboard
an old cargo ship.
When Otto
Preminger offered
him the role,
he accepted it
for $100,000,
half his usual fee.

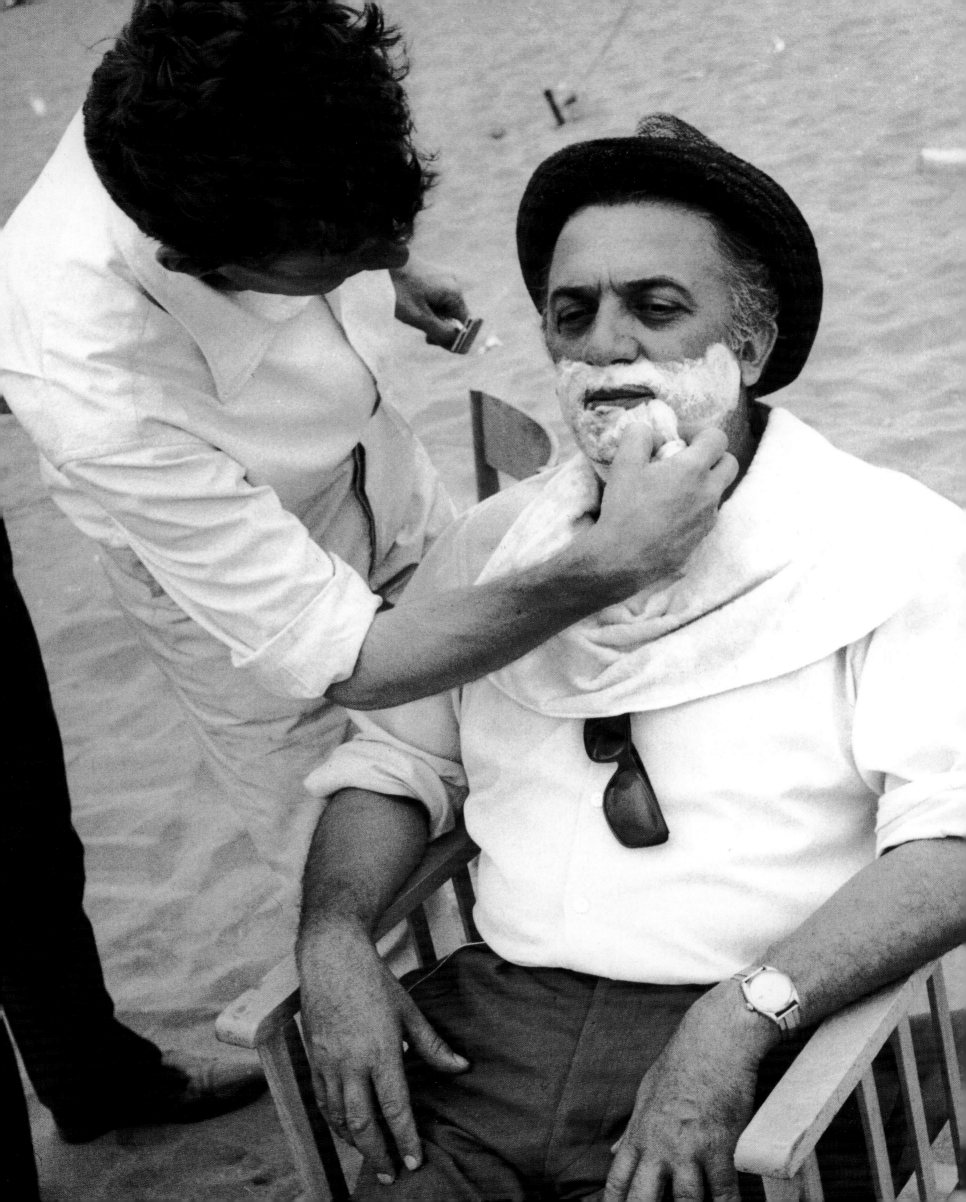

**JULIET OF
THE SPIRITS**
Federico Fellini
1964
Federico Fellini
Each day, the
same ritual
is enacted on the
set: As the film
crew prepares
for the first scene
of the day, the
maestro gets a
shave. "I think
best when I'm
under stress,"
Fellini says.

BALL OF FIRE
Howard Hawks
1941
Gary Cooper
Gary Cooper
distracts himself
while waiting to
work. He has
suffered an eye
irritation and
director Howard
Hawks has
delayed shooting.
The film will finish
one day ahead
of schedule,
as the star and
the director are
both eager to
join Ernest
Hemingway on
a hunting
expedition.

THE WRETCHES
Robert Hossein
1959
Michèle Morgan
Michèle Morgan sits patiently on set while the lighting is adjusted. Robert Hossein had initially promised this role to his wife, Marina Vlady, but they separated before filming began. The film's other leading actress was to be Sylvia Lopez, who passed away unexpectedly prior to the start of filming.

THE GREAT ESCAPE
John Sturges
1962
Steve McQueen
Perched up high, next to a spotlight, Steve McQueen overlooks the stalag, which was re-created near Munich, Germany. He personally customized the motorbike he used for the spectacular chase sequence, and used a stuntman for only a few seconds of the most dangerous parts.

BYE BYE MONKEY
Marco Ferreri
1977
Gérard Depardieu, Marcello Mastroianni
Filmed in New York City, several scenes in *Bye Bye Monkey* take place at the foot of the World Trade Center, next to the carcass of a giant ape that was used a few months earlier in John Guillermin's 1976 remake of *King Kong*.

IT STARTED IN NAPLES
Melville Shavelson
1959
**Sophia Loren,
Clark Gable,
Vittorio De Sica**
Sophia Loren takes her shoes off, De Sica blows his nose, but the "King" is as majestic as always. In her autobiography, Loren relates how Gable once abruptly interrupted a love scene upon hearing the alarm on his watch go off. "This was pure Gable.... He always arrived exactly on time, knew his script by heart, and would leave precisely when his watch declared the hour of five o'clock."

CLEOPATRA
Joseph L. Mankiewicz
1962
Richard Burton
Burton was happily ensconced on Broadway when he was asked to replace Stephen Boyd in the part of Mark Antony in this notoriously troubled film. Twentieth Century Fox was willing to accrue much greater expenses than the relatively minor inconvenience of having to have all Boyd's costumes retailored—the company was forced to pay a hefty amount to all parties concerned in order to cut short Burton's Broadway run.

BONNIE AND CLYDE
Arthur Penn
1967
Faye Dunaway
A few minutes of concentration are often required before a take. Warren Beatty, who produced the film, initially wanted to cast his sister, Shirley MacLaine, as Bonnie. He also considered Carol Linley and Tuesday Weld before finally choosing Faye Dunaway at director Arthur Penn's suggestion. "In the beginning," Penn said "Beatty thought he'd made a mistake, but halfway through the film, he realized that she was just perfect."

CORLEONE
Pasquale Squitieri
1977
Claudia Cardinale
Claudia is relaxed and radiant on the set. This is her third starring role in a film directed by Pasquale Squitieri, a former criminologist (and future senator) who learned his trade by making spaghetti westerns. Two years after shooting this film, the couple will have a daughter together.

WAGES OF FEAR
Henri-Georges Clouzot
1951
Simone Signoret
(left),
Yves Montand
(right)
They are to be
married at the
end of the year,
but will not make
their first film
together until
1956 (*The
Witches of Salem*
by Raymond
Rouleau). In the
summer of 1951,
Simone Signoret,
who is about to
play the lead role
in Jacques
Becker's *Golden
Marie*, visits
Camargue to see
Yves Montand
during the filming
of *Wages of Fear*.
The film was
completed in
the fall of 1952,
and made
multi-talented
Yves a movie star.

THE SIN
Alberto Lattuada
1971
Sophia Loren
For Sophia Loren, acting is about self-discipline. "No matter what emotion is conveyed…or its level of intensity, it is essential to control the situation and not let it overwhelm you."

LIZA
Marco Ferreri
1971
Catherine Deneuve
By the age of twenty-eight, Catherine Deneuve had starred in some thirty films and was already an accomplished actress. But the sudden death of her older sister, Françoise Dorléac, in 1967, was a trauma from which she would never entirely recover. "Both of us together add up to the perfect woman," Françoise had once quipped.

CLEOPATRA
Joseph L. Mankiewicz
1962
A costumed dancer finds shelter from the sun's glare under her Egyptian-esque wing. During filming, costumes and accessories were stolen by the hundreds, and, strangely enough, so were some elephants and tigers.

MY FAIR LADY
George Cukor
1964
The elegant lady with the exuberant hat is an extra in repose. This extraordinary costume, designed by Cecil Beaton, makes it clear why he was awarded an Oscar for Best Costume Design, one of the eight Oscars earned by *My Fair Lady*.

AROUND THE WORLD IN EIGHTY DAYS
Michael Anderson
1955
David Niven
After well over eighty days of filming throughout the world, David Niven has every reason to be tired. This marathon project, which started in Hollywood and stretched over several continents, used local stars for short guest appearances to give the film an atmosphere of authenticity and exoticism.

HIGH SOCIETY
Charles Walters
1956
Charles Walters (back), Frank Sinatra (second from left), Grace Kelly
An exhausted Kelly rests elegantly in her regal chair. This remake of George Cukor's *Philadelphia Story*, where Kelly takes the role Katharine Hepburn immortalized in 1940, will be the first and last time she plays in a musical comedy—she even sings a few bars of "True Love" with Bing Crosby.

MARATHON MAN

John Schlesinger
1976
**Dustin Hoffman,
Laurence Olivier**

Straight from the ranks of the Actors Studio, Dustin Hoffman is the incarnation of a new generation of Hollywood actors. Olivier, reigning star of the Shakespearean repertoire, exemplifies the classic English theatre. But their synergy is perfect. One scene in particular will remain forever etched in viewers' minds: Olivier, playing a former Nazi, tortures his young victim with a dentist's drill to obtain a secret, which, in fact, Hoffman's hapless character does not possess.

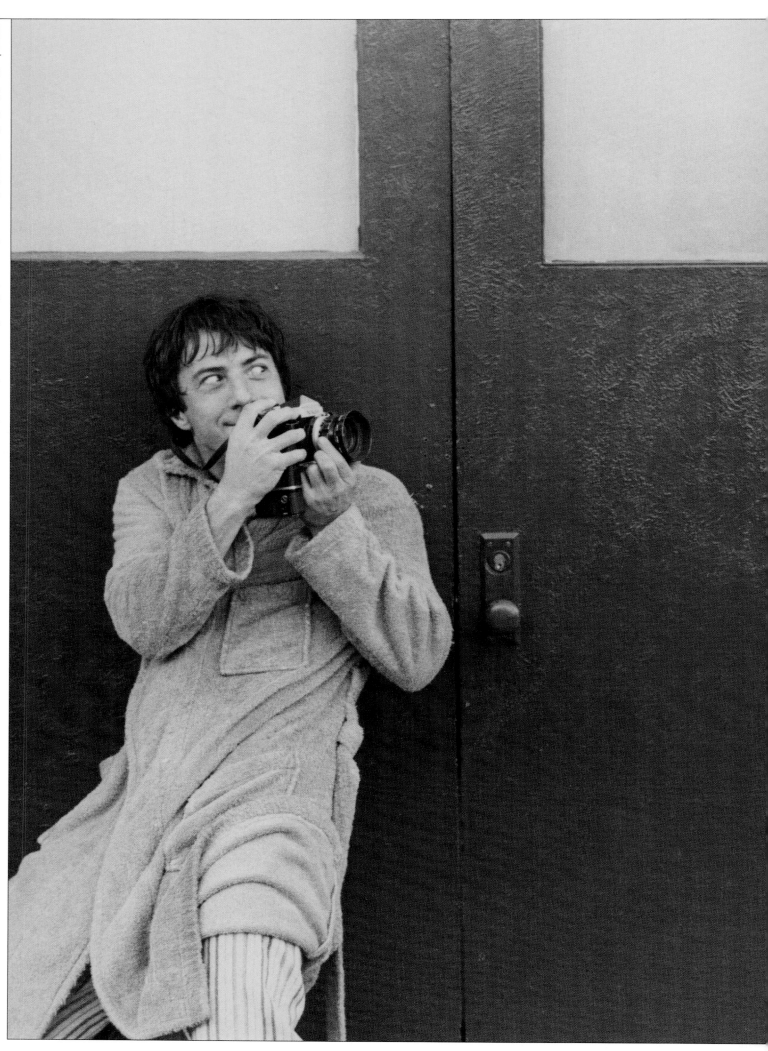

FEVER MOUNTS IN EL PAO
Luis Buñuel
1959
Gérard Philipe, Jean Servais
Two actors document the good times during filming, which started in Mexico City and continued in Mexico's Tepoztlàn region. Gérard Philipe died suddenly of cancer on November 25, 1959, a month and a half before the film was first released in Paris.

MARCO POLO
Christian-Jaque
1962
Alain Delon
A day of leisure in Venice for Alain Delon. The filming of *Marco Polo* will be interrupted by the bankruptcy of producer Raoul J. Lévy. In 1964, Denys de La Patellière and Noël Howard take up the idea once more in *Marco the Magnificent*, with Horst Buchholz playing the intrepid explorer.

CLOAK AND DAGGER
Fritz Lang
1946
Lilli Palmer, Gary Cooper
Does Lilli Palmer really understand how serious her partner Gary Cooper is about this film? Fritz Lang and Cooper thought this movie to be a testament to the dangers of nuclear weapons, but the people at Warner will change the pessimistic ending, which foretold the imminence of a nuclear conflict.

CHIMES AT MIDNIGHT
Orson Welles
1964
Orson Welles
Because of budget restrictions, making this film is an ordeal for Welles. It was interrupted twice, and shooting in Spain had to be done in small sequences over several months. Every night, before getting a few hours of sleep, Welles would prepare his "poor man's studio"—the set he created himself in an old garage. Despite the financial limitations, Welles would on occasion hire hundreds of extras for a few days who would go unused if he found no inspiration.

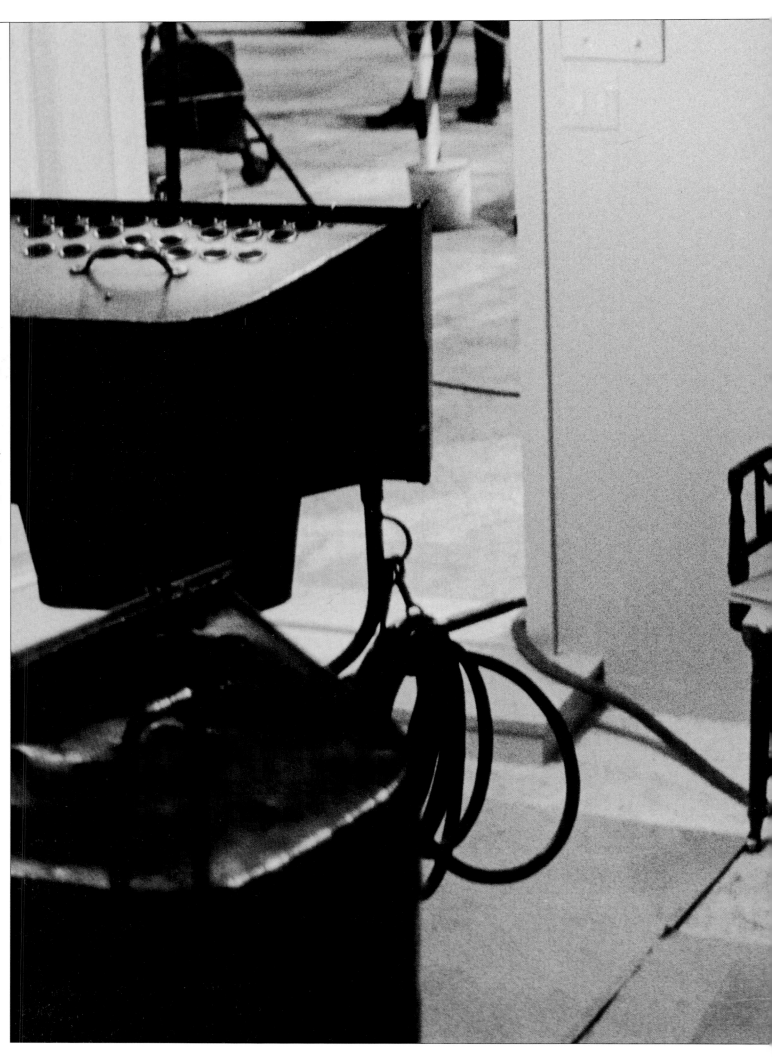

SOMETHING'S GOT TO GIVE
George Cukor
1962
Marilyn Monroe
Feeling weak, and on antidepressants, Marilyn Monroe will never actually play the role she is attempting to learn. Barely ten minutes of footage was shot before the film was abandoned. Monroe died on August 5, 1962 of an apparent overdose. The script was used again in 1963 for Michael Gordon's *More Over Darling*, starring Doris Day. Twentieth Century Fox will use some of the *Something's Got To Give* footage in a documentary called *Marilyn* (1963) and in Michael Sarne's *Myra Breckinridge* (1970).

JUDGMENT AT NUREMBERG
Stanley Kramer
1960
Marlene Dietrich
Although Dietrich hadn't been in a studio for over four years, her militant anti-Nazi stance helped convince her to accept a small role in this 1948 reenactment of the Nuremberg trials. Dietrich plays, with astonishing humanity, the widow of a Third Reich general. "The fact that Spencer Tracy was part of the cast…certainly contributed to my decision," she would later recount in her autobiography. But Tracy's poor health limits filming, leaving Marlene ample time to read *Paris Match*.

WAR AND PEACE
King Vidor
1955
Henry Fonda, Audrey Hepburn
While Audrey Hepburn reads a magazine, Henry Fonda sits in silent consternation. His wife, Anita Ekberg, has just left him after a short-lived marriage. To make matters worse, he doesn't get along with either the producer or the director of the film.

LA DOLCE VITA
Federico Fellini
1959
Marcello Mastroianni, Anita Ekberg, Federico Fellini
Once a comic-book author himself, Fellini was very fond of *fumetti*, a type of Italian comics. He loved to read them off-set while simultaneously keeping an eye on the action. Mastroianni, whom he had chosen over Paul Newman despite the producers' wishes, was to become Fellini's trademark actor.

PATHS OF GLORY
Stanley Kubrick
1957
Adolphe Menjou
The movie was shot in Munich, where Adolphe Menjou, after working so long in Hollywood, could enjoy the European press. Menjou, himself of French origin, is renowned in Hollywood for his flawless elegance, and is nicknamed "the man with the three-hundred suits."

LAWRENCE OF ARABIA
David Lean
1961
Peter O'Toole
After four months baking in the Jordanian desert, filming continues in Spain and Morocco, near Ouarzazate. Peter O'Toole identifies so closely with the character he is playing that he is often completely drained after a scene. Beer, wine and champagne keep him going, but when the waiting gets too long, his excesses occasionally send him off into a deep sleep.

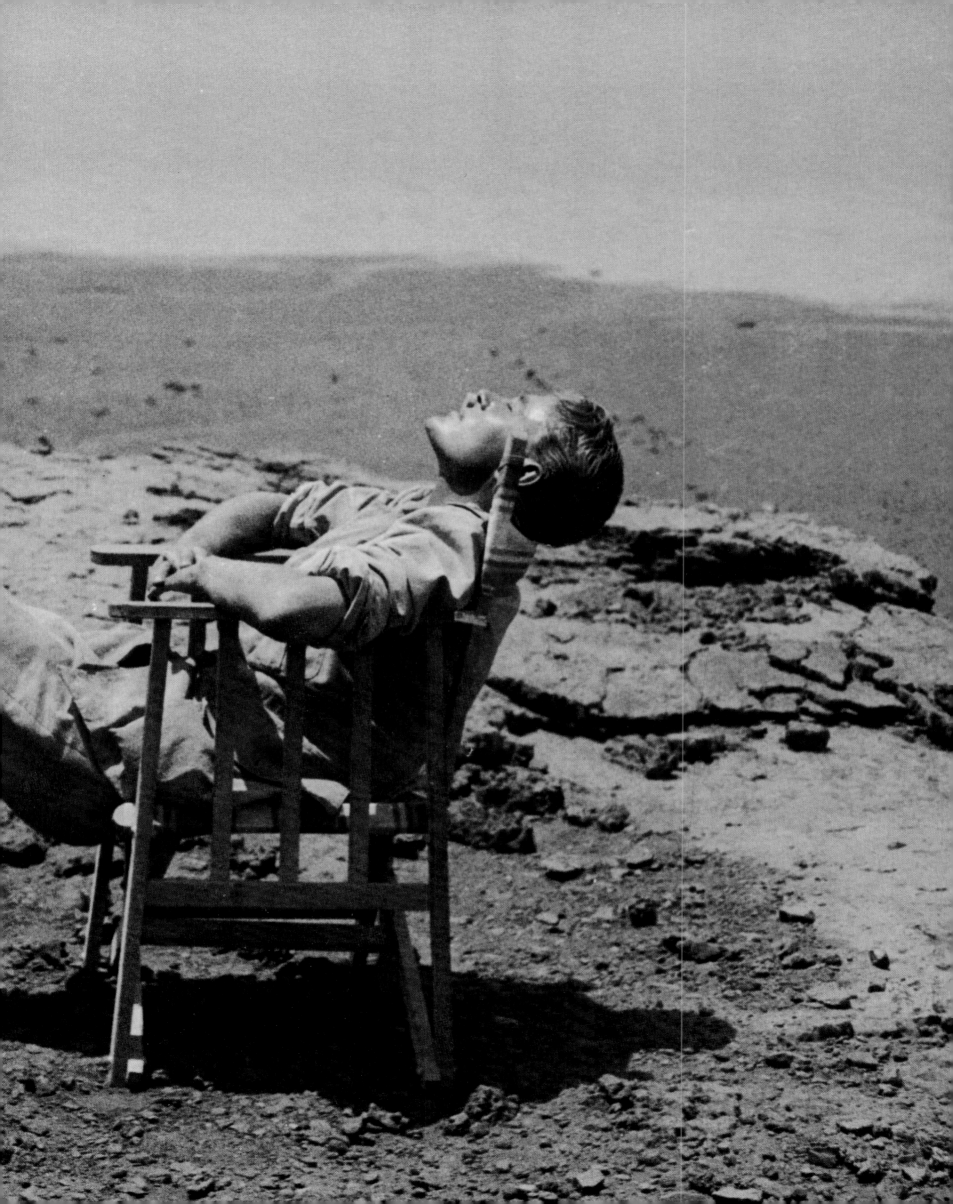

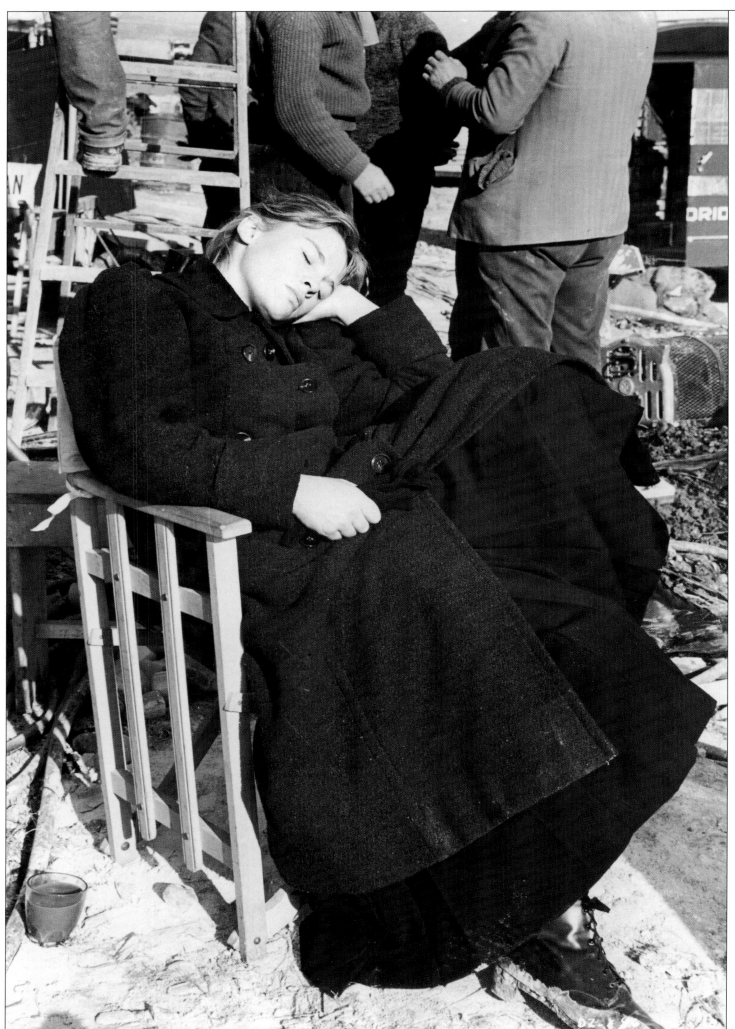

DOCTOR ZHIVAGO
David Lean
1964
Julie Christie
This epic film, shot in Finland and Madrid, was a physical trial for all the actors involved. Despite poor reviews, it will become MGM's biggest commercial success since *Gone With The Wind*, grossing over $100 million at the box office.

THE DAY THE FISH CAME OUT
Michael Cacoyannis
1967
Candice Bergen
This film was an artistic and commercial failure, yet Bergen is bluntly honest about her experience: "It could have been good, but it was a disaster. And I was terrible, just terrible!"

THE BLUE MAX
John Guillermin
1965
Ursula Andress
A Rolls Royce conveys the star's caravan to the tarmac where the next scene is to take place. In this war movie, renowned for its aerial scenes, Ursula Andress plays a German general's wife who falls in love with a young officer. Her passionate love scenes with George Peppard are a prelude to the steamy Italian productions she will later star in. (Photo: C. Azoulay)

THE BAREFOOT CONTESSA
Joseph L. Mankiewicz
1953
Ava Gardner
Ava Gardner's feet were not the only things bruised from her escapades in Spain, while shooting *The Barefoot Contessa*. Her notorious liaison with matador Luis Miguel Dominguin made her husband, Frank Sinatra, so jealous that the couple separated upon the unfaithful beauty's return to America. They finally divorced in 1957.

VIVA MARIA!
Louis Malle
1965
Brigitte Bardot
The star relaxes between takes. Filming in Mexico will last nearly six months, under difficult conditions and in extreme heat. In spite of this, Brigitte Bardot has fond memories of this time. "On set," she says, "I could be a real tomboy, very natural and relaxed...."

THE MAGNIFICENT SEVEN
John Sturges
1959
**Brad Dexter,
Steve McQueen,
James Coburn,
Horst Buchholz,
Yul Brynner**
Out of the seven stars, only Charles Bronson and Robert Vaughn are missing from this photo. In spite of appearances, there is enormous tension between Yul Brynner and Steve McQueen. "We were at odds with each other during the whole shooting…. Yul is a good actor for sure, but when it comes to riding horses or handling guns, he's laughable."

CHISUM
Andrew V. McLaglen
1969
John Wayne
The son of Wayne's old friend Victor McLaglen directs this western produced by Batjac, a company founded by Wayne himself.
Since his lung cancer operation in 1964, the "Duke" has stopped smoking, and only lights up for the camera. Between takes in Mexico, he enjoys a game of chess—a game at which he excels.

THE WILD ONE
Laslo Benedek
1952
Marlon Brando
Inspired by a true story, *The Wild One* is the original motorbike film. It will be banned in England for fourteen years based on assertions that it would incite violence.
During breaks, Brando prefers a chessboard to his hooligan bike.

JUDGMENT AT NUREMBERG
Stanley Kramer
1960
Marlene Dietrich
Surrounded by men in uniform, Marlene Dietrich revels in the atmosphere she first knew during World War II, when she sang for the soldiers. She also enjoys showing the actors and technicians a few card tricks she learned from her friend Orson Welles.

PITTSBURGH
Lewis Seiler
1942
Marlene Dietrich, John Wayne
Costars for the third time, Marlene Dietrich and John Wayne are also lovers. She is the star of the movie, but he is only a featured third after Randolph Scott. Despite the roles given to him by John Ford, he has only played in B movies and is not yet considered a major star.

**FOR WHOM THE
BELL TOLLS**
Sam Wood
**1943
Gary Cooper,
Ingrid Bergman**
This film drags on
for Gary Cooper
—his initial
partner,
Norwegian Vera
Zorina, has been
dismissed after
three weeks, and
all the scenes
must be reshot
with Ingrid
Bergman,
a rising Hollywood
star. Paramount
Pictures, which
just purchased
the rights to
Hemingway's
novel for
$150,000,
initially wanted
Cecil B. DeMille
to direct, but
eventually settled
for his assistant
Sam Wood.

THE GUNS OF NAVARONE
J. Lee Thompson
1961
**Stanley Baker,
Gregory Peck,
Anthony Quinn,
David Niven**
A game of chess between two gentlemen: These prestigious international stars are working together for the first time on this World War II drama. Directed by Englishman Jack Lee Thompson, the scenes are filmed in Greece on the island of Rhodes.

THE NIGHT OF THE GENERALS
Anatole Litvak
1965
Peter O'Toole
Although this is a cosmopolitan production—filmed in Paris with a director of Russian origin—it is still surprising to see Anglo-Irish Peter O'Toole, in full Nazi attire, playing the traditional American sport of baseball during breaks.
(Photo: C. Azoulay)

THE GREEK TYCOON
J. Lee Thompson
1978
Anthony Quinn
Anthony Quinn plays a wealthy, Greek shipping tycoon in love with the widow of an assassinated American President. His character is much more interested in business and women than in chess. It would be a bit of a stretch to say that the inspiration for this script was purely imaginary.

ONE NIGHT...
A TRAIN
André Delvaux
1968
Yves Montand,
Pierre Barouh,
Anouk Aimée
Pierre Barouh and
Anouk Aimée
have been
romantically
linked since
Claude Lelouch's
*A Man and
A Woman* (1967).
Barouh came to
Belgium to see
her act with Yves
Montand, who
has invited him to
play a game of
cards while
Aimée sits
nearby,
engrossed in a
comic book.
Montand must
speak Flemish in
several scenes,
but his accent is
terrible and will
provoke much
laughter in
Belgium.

MARIE-ANTOINETTE, QUEEN OF FRANCE
Jean Delannoy
1955
Michèle Morgan
As the French say, "one must suffer to be beautiful." Director Jean Delannoy is notoriously fastidious about details, especially those regarding costumes. He is less interested in historic accuracy than in elegant effects, and the French New Wave would later mock this type of academic approach as too affected.

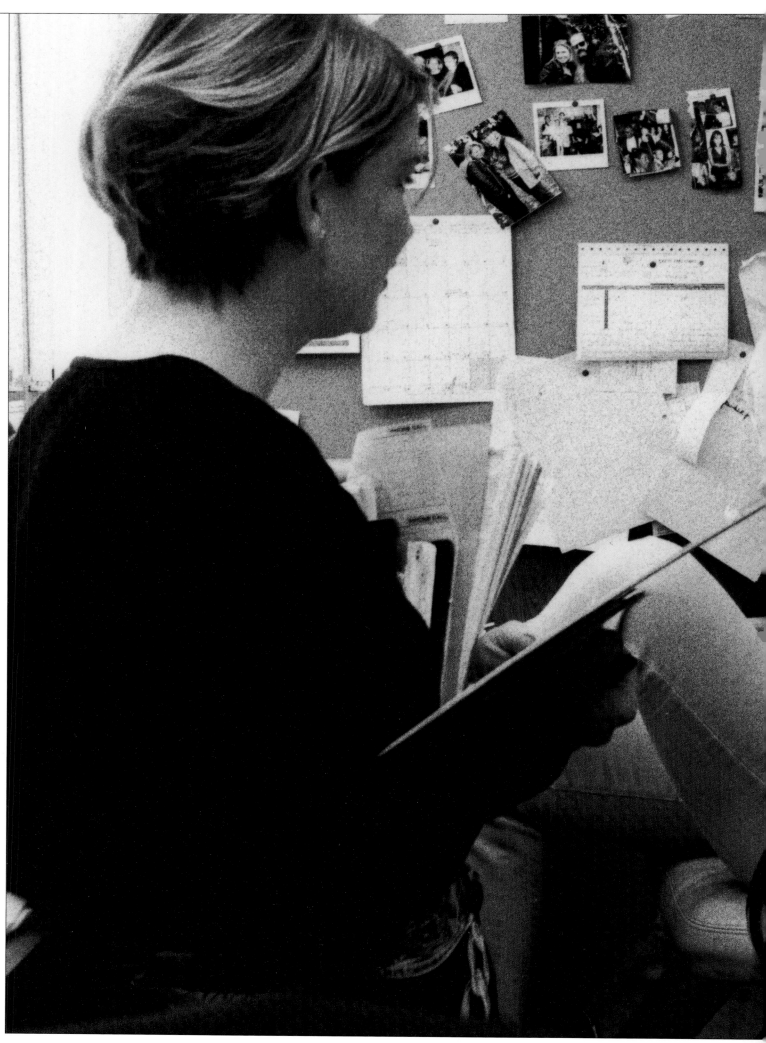

SLIVER
Phillip Noyce
1992
Sharon Stone
Sharon Stone is being groomed in her dressing room. The scandalous success of Paul Verhoeven's *Basic Instinct* has made her one of the most sought-after stars in the world, capable of earning $10 million a film. But her stormy relations with costar, William Baldwin, make things difficult for Phillip Noyce, who is himself in open conflict with another leading actor, Tom Berenger. The previews are so bad that the producers will force Noyce to shoot three different endings.

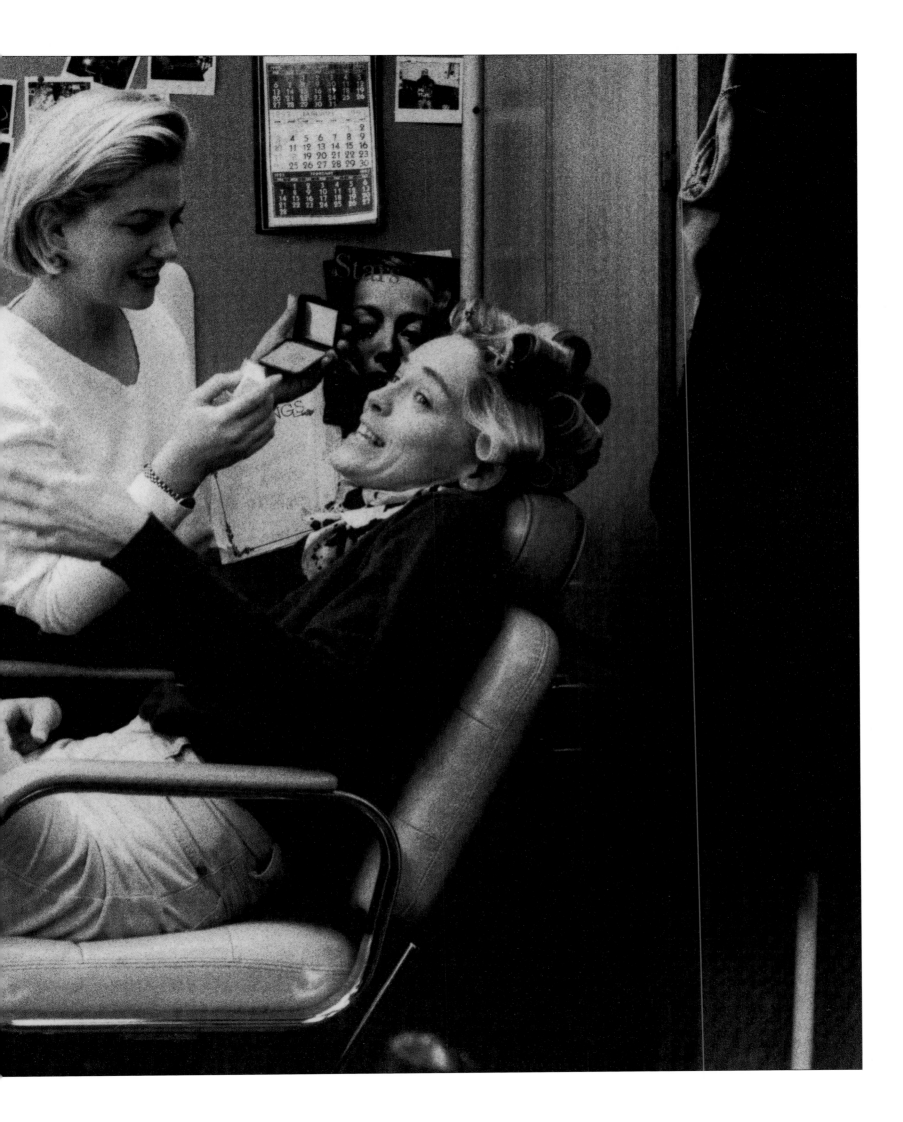

HIGH SOCIETY
Charles Walters
1956
Charles Walters (back to the camera), Grace Kelly
The star reapplies her lipsticks while taking in the director's instructions. Under contract to Metro Goldwyn Mayer, this is Grace Kelly's last film before her marriage to Prince Rainier of Monaco. Ten years later, she would appear in her very last film, Terence Young's *The Poppy Is Also a Flower*, as herself, the Princess of Monaco.

BEAUTIES OF THE NIGHT
René Clair
1952
Martine Carol
Costume designer Rosine Delamare can rest assured that Martine Carol won't wrinkle her dress. A special vertical chair with armrests, but no seat, was created so Carol could relax comfortably in an upright position between takes.

THE BLUE MAX
John Guillermin
1965
Ursula Andress
The gown worn by Ursula Andress was designed by newcomer John Furniss, who will later work with the likes of Don Chaffey, John Huston, Joseph Losey, Sidney Gilliat, Joseph L. Mankiewicz, Peter Duffell and Peter Bogdanovich. (Photo: C. Azoulay)

HIGH SOCIETY
Charles Walters
1956
**Grace Kelly,
William Tuttle
(right)**
Grace Kelly is
in her dressing
room preparing
for a scene.
While last-
minute
adjustments are
done on her hair,
William Tuttle,
who heads the
makeup
department at
MGM, is making
sure that her
touch-up won't
reflect under
the spotlights.

THE TEN COMMANDMENTS
Cecil B. DeMille
1954
At the foot of a plaster sphinx, the hair and makeup people are overwhelmed with extras. On a panel hang dozens of fake beards that eerily resemble scalps. Close by, the actors' legs are darkened with a paint pistol.

THE LONGEST DAY
Darryl F. Zanuck
1962
Darryl F. Zanuck
Reputed to be both a shrewd and tyrannical producer, Zanuck considers this film the crowning achievement of his career. He is everywhere at once, coordinating the different teams, and often personally taking care of minute details to ensure that he gets exactly what he wants.

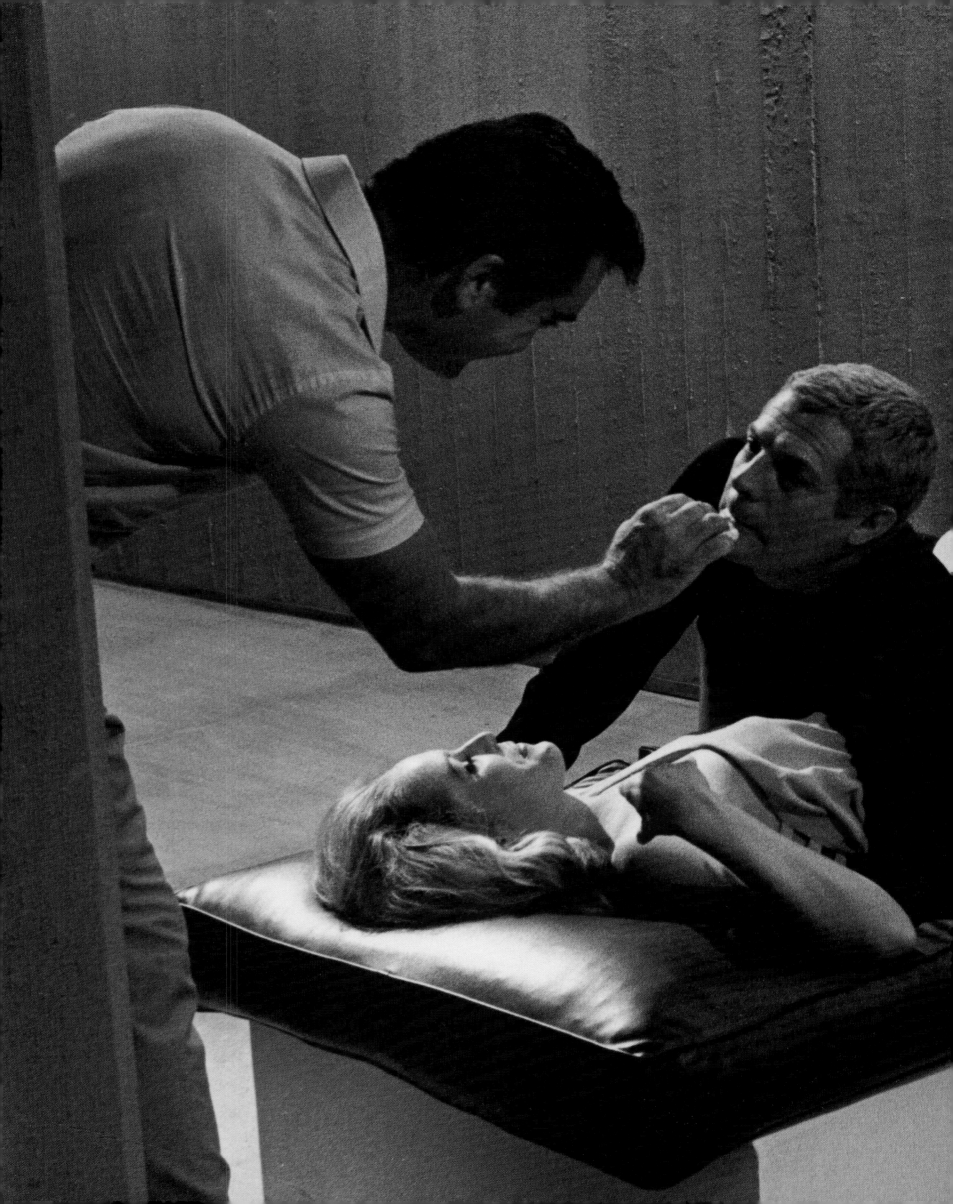

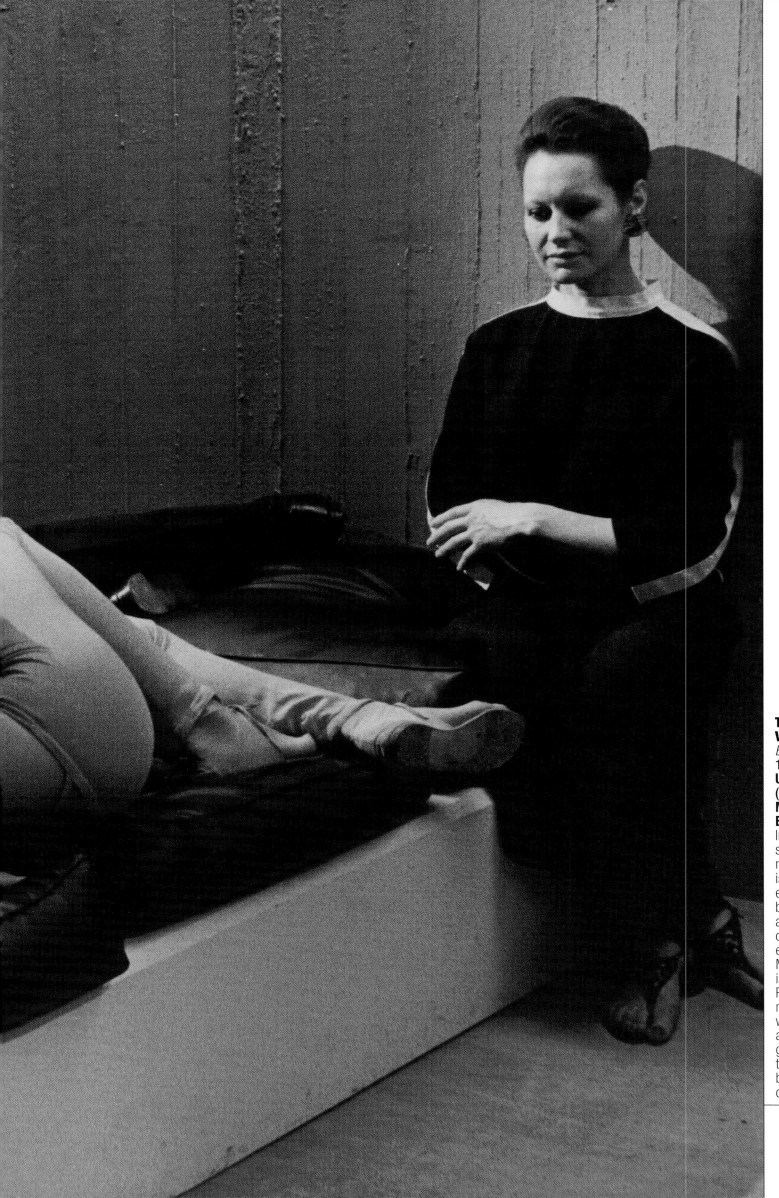

THE TENTH VICTIM
Elio Petri
1965
Ursula Andress (lying), Marcello Mastroianni, Elsa Martinelli
In this stylish, science-fiction movie (the action is set in 1977), everyone in turn becomes hunter and hunted—at one point Ursula even goes after Marcello. The film is inspired by a Robert Sheckley novel, and after watching it, the author himself gets inspiration to write another book—based on the film!

BARBARELLA
Roger Vadim
1967
Jane Fonda, Roger Vadim
Barbarella was based on Claude Forest's comic strips about a sexy space vixen. It attempts to capture the original's visual fantasy. Married to Vadim since 1965, Jane Fonda refused the leading role in *Rosemary's Baby* to star in the film. The imaginative costumes were designed by Jacques Fontenay and Paco Rabanne.

CHIMES AT MIDNIGHT
Orson Welles
1964
Orson Welles
No makeup staff for Orson Welles. With a budget of only $800,000, he must count every penny. For the major roles, known actors are hired for a few days only and are replaced by doubles as soon as they are not facing the camera.

Under The
Spotlight

or "Silence on the Set"

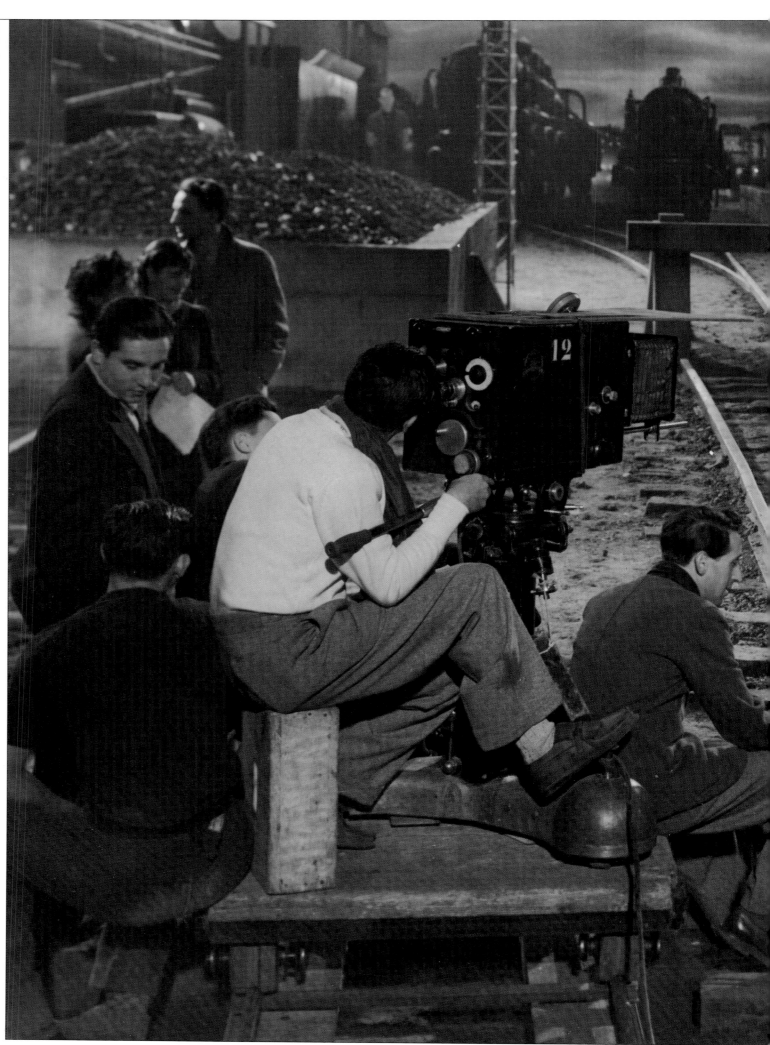

THE HUMAN BEAST
Jean Renoir
1938
**Jean Gabin,
Simone Simon,
Jean Renoir
(to the right,
with hat)**
Jean Renoir loved actors, and the actors who played in his films all revered him. Before starring as a railroad worker in this film based on the novel by Emile Zola, Jean Gabin learns how to drive a real train. "If only Zola could see it," Renoir once said. "He would be very pleased."

INTERVISTA
Federico Fellini
1986
**Federico Fellini,
Anita Ekberg**
Fellini declared:
"I never moralize.
I'm not qualified
for that; I'm not a
censor, a priest,
nor a politician.
I don't like to
analyze myself;
I don't deliver
speeches, I'm not
a philosopher,
nor have I any
theories. I'm a
storyteller,
making movies
is my job."

THE TEN COMMANDMENTS
Cecil B. DeMille
1954
Cecil B. DeMille
Perched next to a camera during a take in the Sinai desert south of Cairo, DeMille is directing the remake of his 1923 silent movie masterpiece. Filming will take one full year, in studios in Hollywood and in Paris, cost $13 million, employ over twelve-hundred actors, and bring in over $80 million at the box office.

ONCE UPON A TIME IN THE WEST
Sergio Leone
1968
Sergio Leone
Sergio Leone is seen filming with a light camera while sitting on the shoulders of one of his assistants. This will be his fourth spaghetti western and is shot in the Almeria desert in Spain. "John Ford is a filmmaker I deeply respect," says Leone. "He is the reason I make westerns."

ROCCO AND HIS BROTHERS

Luchino Visconti

1960
Luchino Visconti, Alain Delon

In 1958, Visconti planned on casting Delon as the Rocco character. But it took two more years to perfect the script and to find financing. The film, shot in Milan, is organized around the French actor, whom the director managed to hire despite his initially skeptical producers. Accused of being obscene when it first opened in Italy, it soon became a classic and confirmed Delon's star status.

BOOM!
Joseph Losey
1968
Joseph Losey
(bare chested),
Elizabeth Taylor
(standing in
middle),
Michael Dunn
(to the right)
This film is
plagued from the
beginning—from
a severe storm
and a fire, to the
plunge of Liz
Taylor's trailer
(without Liz) off a
high cliff. But it
would have taken
a lot more than
that to destroy the
diva's happiness
—Richard
Burton, her costar
and husband, has
just given her the
Krupp Diamond,
the largest
diamond in the
world.

TO CATCH A THIEF
Alfred Hitchcock
1955
Alfred Hitchcock

"I'm against virtuosity," Hitchcock says. In his mind, the function of technique is strictly to serve the story. "The only question I ask myself is where a camera should be placed to add power to the scene. Every element, including the inherent beauty of the picture, the aesthetics of the movements, the rhythms and the effects, must all be used for the purpose of the action."

CHIMES AT MIDNIGHT
Orson Welles
1964
Orson Welles

If Orson Welles always had questions about his actors, or about the script itself, he is never in doubt when it comes to framing a shot. "I usually place my camera intuitively. If this doesn't happen right away, that means that I just don't know how to film the scene, or that I am going in a wrong direction."

PINOCCHIO
*Ben Sharpsteen,
Hamilton Luske*
1937
Walt Disney
In the same year
that his legendary
*Snow White and
the Seven
Dwarves* was
released, Disney
began work on
this adaptation of
Collodi's famous
book. Real actors
are filmed in
stop-action
to serve as
models for the
characters, and
a marionette
is used to play
Pinocchio.
For nearly three
years, a team
of twelve hundred
people work
on this project,
but Walt Disney
himself ultimately
controlled every
detail of its
production.

MOBY DICK
John Huston
1956
**Gregory Peck,
John Huston**
Making a movie out of this famous book was a pet project for John Huston, who saw in his own father the perfect Ahab. But when Walter Huston died in 1950, Gregory Peck was chosen to play the relentless sea captain. The film was shot in several locations, including the Azores, the Canary Islands, Wales and a London studio.

ANTONY AND CLEOPATRA
Charlton Heston
1972
Charlton Heston
Heston strongly identified with the character of Mark Antony, Caesar's top lieutenant and lover of Cleopatra. He had already played roles in two adaptations of Shakespeare's *Julius Caesar* (in 1950 under the direction of David Bradley, and in 1970 with Stuart Burge) and would direct and star in his own attempt at Shakespeare. Filmed in Spain, *Antony and Cleopatra* will be a fiasco. But this won't discourage Heston, who consoles himself by directing a western in 1982 (*Mother Lode*) and a film for television in 1988 (*A Man For All Seasons*).

APOCALYPSE NOW
Francis Ford Coppola
1978
Francis Ford Coppola
"This film is not about Vietnam," Coppola said. "It *is* Vietnam. I wanted America to look straight into the face of horror and see its own reflection." The film, shot in the Philippines, had to overcome several catastrophes—an earthquake, two typhoons, the dismissal of the main actor (Harvey Keitel) and his replacement Martin Sheen's heart attack. "Little by little, we were all becoming mad," Coppola confessed.

PLAY TIME
Jacques Tati
1967
Jacques Tati
After a ten-year absence Monsieur Hulot is back. For Tati, a good comedy is much more than performing comical antics in front of the camera—he understood the importance of each detail, gesture, camera angle, and sound. "I don't think comedy is simply a funny face behind a camera and an exaggerated mannerism," he said while making the first Hulot film, *My Uncle* (1958).

GIGOT
Gene Kelly
1962
**Diane Gardner,
Gene Kelly**
(in the hat),
Jean Bourgoin
(behind the
camera)
Belleville, the
popular old
district of Paris
where the outdoor
scenes for
this film were
shot, will be
demolished in the
decade following.
As for the film,
the producers
perpetrated their
own demolition
before its release.
"When I saw it in
New York," Gene
Kelly said, "it had
nothing to do with
the version I
initially did. I was
never consulted
and never knew
who had
truncated it."

RAIDERS OF THE LOST ARK
Steven Spielberg
1981
Steven Spielberg
Like Gulliver in a Lilliputian world, Steven Spielberg looks over a miniature set to prepare his scenes. This will be his first collaboration with producer George Lucas, who originally suggested the idea. Filmed in England, France, Tunisia and Hawaii, it will cost $20 million, but will gross ten times more at the box office.

RAGING BULL
Martin Scorsese
1980
Robert De Niro,
Jake La Motta,
Martin Scorsese
With his
encyclopedic
knowledge of film
and his love
of the sport,
Scorsese knows
how powerful
a boxing movie
can be.
To play the role
of Jake La
Motta—the world
middleweight
champion
between 1949
and 1951—
Robert De Niro
gained 80
pounds.
La Motta was
impressed by
De Niro's
performance,
being an actor
himself—
La Motta was
featured in Robert
Rossen's *The
Hustler* (1961),
Herb Stanley's
*Confessions of
a Psycho Cat*
(1968), Michael
Winner's
Firepower (1979)
and William
Lustig's *Maniac
Cop* (1988).

THE BIRDS
Alfred Hitchcock
1963
Alfred Hitchcock
(left)
The more the merrier: these dummy crows are intended to attract the real thing. Hitchcock employed the services of Ray Berwick, an animal trainer who became famous from the TV series *Lassie*. The scenes of birds swarming the screen were animated with the help of Ub Iwerks, who created the Mickey Mouse character for Walt Disney thirty-five years earlier.

CLEOPATRA
Joseph L. Mankiewicz
1962
Rex Harrison, Elizabeth Taylor, Joseph L. Mankiewicz (back turned, center)
"My next film will take place in a phone booth with two actors and will last five minutes," exclaims an exasperated Mankiewicz on the gigantic set. Exhausted by the difficulties and the length of the filming, and disgusted by his bitter conflicts with the producers, he will only refer to Cleopatra as, "the film whose title I never mention."

THE SEVEN YEAR ITCH
Billy Wilder
1955
Tom Ewell, Marilyn Monroe
On 52nd Street in New York City, thousands of bystanders gape as a draft from a street grate lifts Marilyn's skirt. The public spectacle caused by this sequence will make Monroe's husband, baseball star Joe DiMaggio, extremely jealous. "Everyone wanted to see the wind lift up her skirt," remembers Wilder. "But there wasn't the slightest draft, even when the subway drove by. We had to install six big ventilators…. In the end, the scene was re-shot in a studio."

CONQUEST
Clarence Brown
1937
Clarence Brown (sitting, left), Charles Boyer, Greta Garbo
"The Divine," Greta Garbo, is tired of her usual roles, if not of the movie business altogether. *Conquest*, in which she plays Napoleon's (Charles Boyer) mistress, will be her last drama. She will play in two more comedies, Ernst Lubitsch's *Ninotchka* (1939) and George Cukor's *Two-Faced Woman* (1941), before retiring, at the age of 36, at the height of her fame.

THE FALL OF THE ROMAN EMPIRE

Anthony Mann
1963
Sophia Loren (left), Anthony Mann

After making several great westerns, Anthony Mann is nearing the end of an illustrious career when he agrees to direct two epic movies—*El Cid* (1961) and *The Fall of the Roman Empire*—for the eccentric producer Samuel Bronston. The shooting takes place in Spain, where Bronston builds gigantic studios. The high point of the movie will be the chariot race, conceived by Andrew Marton and Yakima Canut—who had already orchestrated this type of scene for *Ben Hur* (1958).

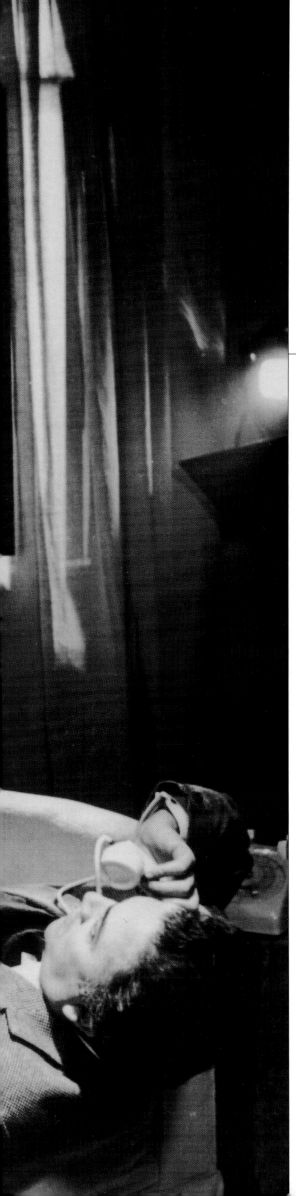

LA DOLCE VITA
Federico Fellini
1959
Marcello Mastroianni, Federico Fellini
"Fellini never asks me to think about a character," Marcello Mastroianni once declared. "He knows that I am at his disposal and he can therefore ask me to do anything he wants." The director is seen showing the actor the posture he's looking for in this scene. Mastroianni willingly obliges.

**THE PARADINE
CASE**
Alfred Hitchcock
1947
Alfred Hitchcock
Although he does
his best to direct
them, certain
actors chosen
by producer
O. Selznick, who
also wrote the
script, do not
please Hitchcock
at all. He initially
wanted Laurence
Olivier, Greta
Garbo and Robert
Newton,
but ended up with
Gregory Peck,
Alida Valli and
Louis Jourdain
instead. "In a
documentary,
God is the
director. But in a
fiction the director
is God, for he
must create life."

GUYS AND DOLLS
Joseph L. Mankiewicz
1955
Michael Kidd, Marlon Brando

Mankiewicz chose Brando over Gene Kelly to sing and dance with Sinatra. "I accepted the part," Brando said "because I believe an actor should never turn down an opportunity to learn something new." Michael Kidd, the film's choreographer, who strikingly resembles Frank Sinatra, gets along much better with Brando during a dance rehearsal than Sinatra ever would. Sinatra, infuriated by Brando's long conversations with Mankiewicz, nicknames him "the mumbler." Knowing how much Sinatra hated redoing a scene, Brando would systematically ask Mankiewicz to shoot several takes. At the end of filming they are no longer on speaking terms.

THE JOURNEY
Anatole Litvak
1958
**Yul Brynner,
Anatole Litvak**
The work seems more like fun: Litvak shows Brynner the proper way to dance a mazurka. The film is set in Hungary, but is actually shot in Austria with an international cast including stars from the U.S., Great Britain, Austria, Germany and France.

WEST SIDE STORY
Robert Wise and Jerome Robbins
1961
A scene shot in the streets of New York City where the Sharks and the Jets rumbled. *West Side Story*, which won ten Academy Awards, is a film adaptation of the 1957 Broadway show choreographed by Jerome Robbins. Robbins worked for a full year preparing the dance scenes with Robert Wise, leaving it to him to actually direct the filming itself.

WAR AND PEACE
King Vidor
1955
Following the success of his blockbuster film *Ulysses*, producer Dino DeLaurentiis wanted to again use director Mario Camerini and actors Kirk Douglas and Silvana Mangano, DeLaurentiis's wife. Camerini preferred Audrey Hepburn, who, in turn, insisted upon her husband, Mel Ferrer, as her leading man. After all that, the coproducers in Hollywood decided that they didn't want an Italian director and ditched Camerini for King Vidor. Planes were used for aerial shots of the battle scenes.

SPARTACUS
Stanley Kubrick
1960
**Kirk Douglas,
Woody Strode,
Stanley Kubrick
(sitting to the
right, half
hidden)**
Kirk Douglas,
who produced
this ambitious
saga, dismissed
director Anthony
Mann after just
one week and
replaced him with
Stanley Kubrick.
Written by Dalton
Trumbo (recently
blacklisted for
his communist
convictions),
the film will cost
$12 million—
three times the
initial budget.

THE LONGEST DAY
Darryl F. Zanuck
1962
**Peter Lawford
(first row, in white)**
Directed by no less than five filmmakers under the supervision of Darryl F. Zanuck, this great World War II epic, depicting the 1944 landing of Allied troops in Normandy, has an impressive cast of over fifty American, British, French and German stars, including mega-star John Wayne.

BARABBAS
Richard Fleischer
1962
The actors hanging from crosses in the foreground of this collective crucifixion scene must be untied between takes to drink and rest. In the background, dummies are used instead of actors.

AUSTERLITZ
Abel Gance
1960
A lyrical
Abel Gance
prophesized:
"I can predict
delirious
enthusiasm,
like the tragic
Greek authors
might have
experienced
in the arenas
of their time
in front of twenty
thousand
breathless
spectators.
Whether we like
it or not, films
are becoming
fantastic
shows where
the collective
psyche will be
imprinted by
this popular art."

FRIC-FRAC
Maurice Lehmann
1939
Michel Simon
Michel Simon plays the role of a lovable thief and master of his own personal argot that he perfected in the theatre. He's wonderful, as always, but his relations with costar Fernandel were less than stellar. "It's a pity that these two great personalities didn't get along. Fernandel never wanted to work with Simon again," opined Arletty, their partner in the film.

THE LAW
Jules Dassin
1958
Yves Montand, Jules Dassin
The indoor scenes were shot in Paris, the outdoor scenes in Italy. Yves Montand remembers director Jules Dassin telling the producer: "Either we hire Montand or I won't do the film at all."

FANTASTIC VOYAGE
Richard Fleischer
1965
Five scientists, reduced to microscopic size, explore the inside of a human body. The gigantic sets, more dreamlike than realistic, are made of fiberglass and flexible resins, and provide the movie's main attraction. This capillary vein alone is 36 yards long, the heart 50 yards and the brain nearly 80 yards long.

THE SICILIAN CLAN
Henri Verneuil
1969
One of the main scenes takes place in a hijacked Boeing jet. Instead of renting an actual plane, which is both expensive and not very practical for filming, Verneuil asked his chief decorator, Jacques Saulnier, to reconstruct a life-size cockpit in the studio. (Photo: C. Azoulay)

WAGES OF FEAR
Henri-Georges Clouzot
1952
Henri-Georges Clouzot
The director is preparing a scene where Charles Vanel—pinned by tree branches in the middle of a large puddle of oil—has his legs crushed when their truck, driven by Yves Montand, bears down on him. Thousands of gallons of black water are used to hide the platform designed to ensure the actor's safety.

WITNESS IN THE CITY
Edouard Molinaro
1959
Lino Ventura
In the final scene, Lino Ventura is riddled by machine-gun fire. To simulate the impact of bullets, small explosives are hidden under his clothes and the cables are cropped out of the scene.
In following years, a wireless system is invented, where just the sound of gunshots is enough to detonate these tiny explosions.

**MORE THAN
A MIRACLE**
Francesco Rosi
1966
**Omar Sharif,
Sophia Loren**
Sophia Loren
is a poor peasant
girl running
barefoot with
Omar Sharif,
the prince whose
heart many
jealous rivals are
trying to capture.
Her flight takes
place outdoors
on rocky terrain,
which Loren
endures without
complaint. But
her bruised feet
are testimony to
the treachery of
the scene.

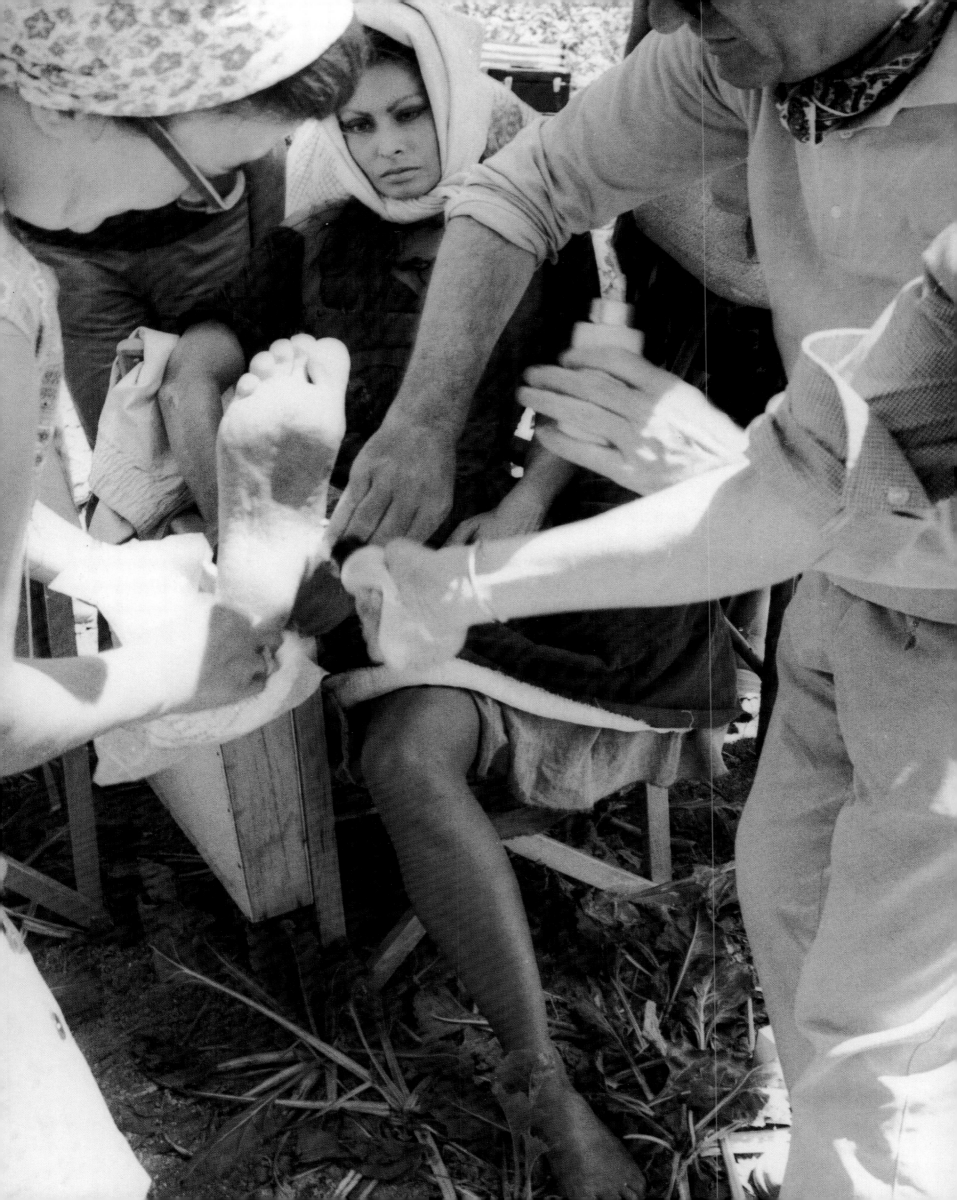

**FAMOUS LOVE
AFFAIRS**
Michel Boisrond
1961
**Brigitte Bardot,
Alain Delon**
In the first of
two water scenes,
Brigitte Bardot
swims nude
to seduce
Alain Delon.
In the second,
she is sentenced
to death for
witchcraft
and thrown in
the water with
a stone around
her neck to
drown along
with Delon,
whose heroic
attempts to save
her have failed.
A tense moment
ensues when
the studio
technicians
wrongly adjust
the flow of the
artificial river's
current and the
two stars must
be rescued.

THE FOXIEST GIRL IN PARIS
Christian-Jaque
1957
Left page:
**Martine Carol,
Michel Piccoli**
Right page:
**Martine Carol,
Jean Gillet,
Christian-Jaque
(kneeling right)**
"I had to do a judo move on Martine Carol," Piccoli recalls. "But she fell badly, severely injuring her back...." Jean Gillet, Carol's judo instructor, realigns her vertebrae on the set, but she requires hospitalization because of torn ligaments. As a result, filming will be suspended for three months. The following year, she will divorce director Christian-Jaque, her husband since 1954.

FATHOM

Leslie Martinson

1966

Raquel Welch

During a swimming scene, Raquel Welch develops severe cramps, but her cries for help are interpreted as part of the script. Finally, a savvy technician standing by realizes her plight, dives in and brings the shivering star to safety. This James Bond-like spy thriller was shot in Spain's Costa Brava.

THE AFRICAN QUEEN

John Huston

1951

Humphrey Bogart

Although some sequences were filmed in a London studio, the main scenes are shot in Belgian Congo and in Uganda. A doctor measures Bogie and Huston's blood pressure every morning, even though they are the only two members of the team not to be stricken by either dysentery or malaria. As Katharine Hepburn notes in her book on this epic film: "Those two had so much alcohol in their system no germ could possibly survive there."

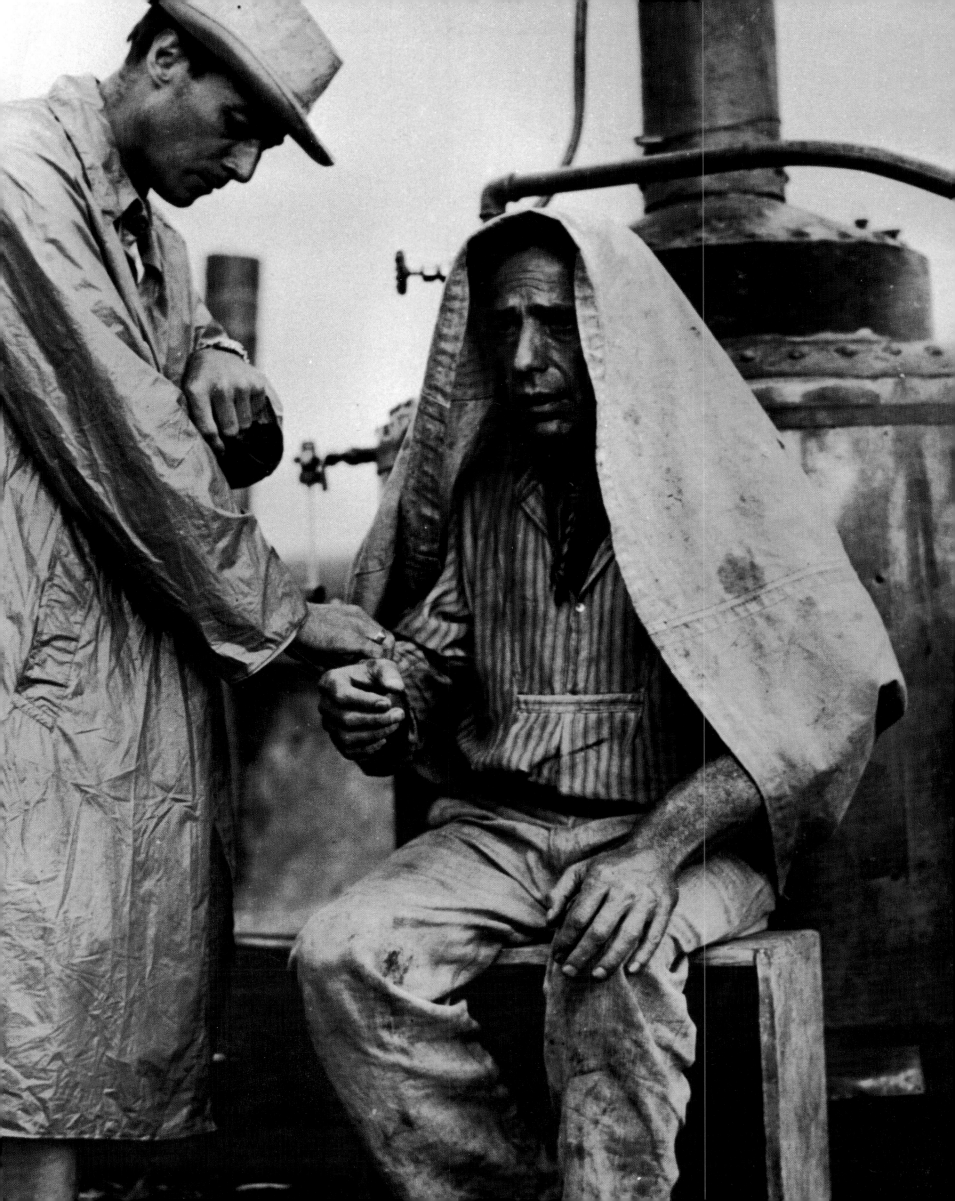

SUMMERTIME
David Lean
1955
Katharine Hepburn
An impromptu drama: One moment of inattention, one wrong move from Gaitano Andiero (Katharine Hepburn's young Venetian escort in the film) and Hepburn is caught off balance, inadvertently plunging into the water. Hepburn received an Oscar nomination for her performance, but her fall in the polluted waters of the lagoon left her with an eye infection that would trouble her for the rest of her life.

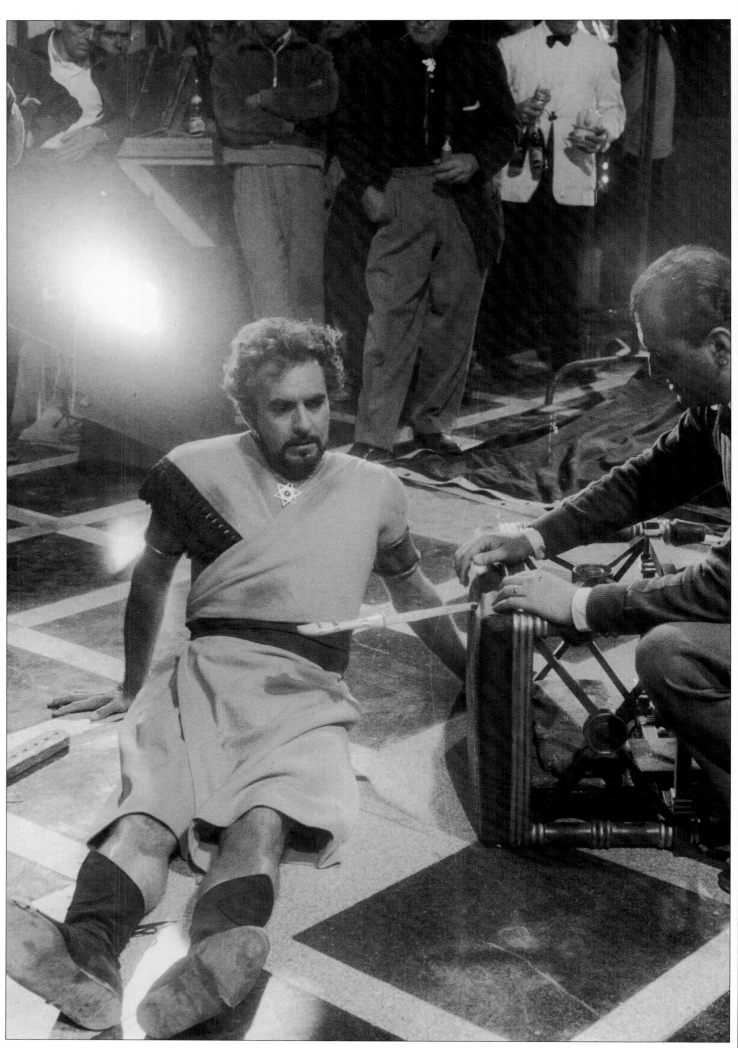

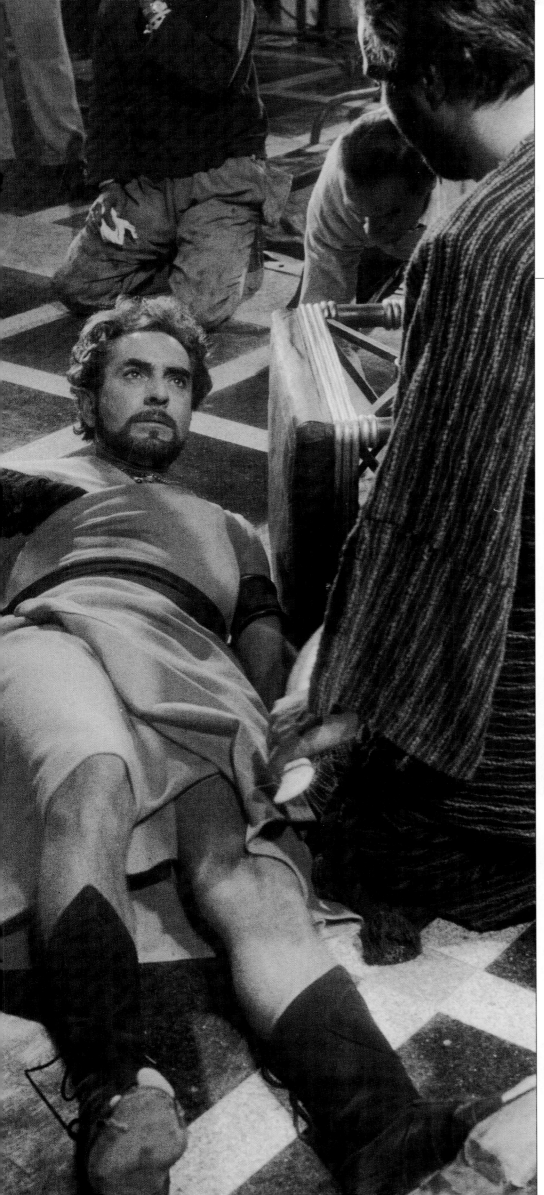

SOLOMON AND SHEBA
King Vidor
1958
Tyrone Power

This scene was shot in Madrid on November 15, 1958, the day of Tyrone Power's death. During a duel scene between Power and George Sanders, Power suddenly collapses from a heart attack, plunging his dagger into a chair that topples with him as he falls. Hours later, he will die in the hospital at the age of forty-five. Power's body is flown back to the United States for burial. The half-finished film was entirely redone with newly recruited Yul Brynner, who will arrive only six days after this tragic incident. Power's trailer will never be occupied again.

We Loved Each Other

So Much

or Intimate Moments

THE SICILIAN CLAN
Henri Verneuil
1969
Lino Ventura,
Jean Gabin,
Alain Delon
Starring in his last gangster movie, Jean Gabin finds himself working with two actors whom he greatly admires— Lino Ventura who made his debut appearance with Gabin in Jacques Becker's *Grisbi* (1953), and Alain Delon who had starred with Gabin in Verneuil's *Any Number Can Win* (1963).
"It was a real pleasure seeing these three sitting at the same table. They would gorge themselves and joke around like a bunch of kids, but as soon as Gabin started talking, Lino and Alain would stop and listen to the boss."

THE WRATH OF GOD
Ralph Nelson
1972
Rita Hayworth (sitting, forefront)
The former sex symbol seems solitary and reflective during her lunch break. She is unhappy with the mediocrity of her last few movies and is fighting depression and the illness that will eventually claim her life. This is to be her last movie; she will retire at the age of fifty-three. Hayworth began her acting career at the age of seventeen as Rita Cansino, dancing a scorching tango in Harry Lachman's *Dante's Inferno* (1935).

TO CATCH A THIEF
Alfred Hitchcock
1955
Roland Lesaffre, Grace Kelly
When you're spoon-fed, you don't come to the table, the table comes to you. "Everyone was dazzled by her elegance, her unaffected gracefulness and her smooth, dancer's gait. She had an amazing charm which she used artfully," remembers Lesaffre about Kelly.

THE YOUNG LIONS
Edward Dmytryk
1957
Marlon Brando
Brando, in full Nazi regalia, appreciates fine French wines, as did the Germans who occupied France during the War. As soon as the film wraps, he will marry a beautiful young Indian woman named Anna Kashfi. Fond of exotic beauties, a disappointed Brando will divorce her soon after he finds out she is of Irish descent.

TO CATCH A THIEF
Alfred Hitchcock
1954
Grace Kelly, Alfred Hitchcock
In the high British tradition, Alfred Hitchcock has a cup of tea with his actors every day at five sharp. *To Catch a Thief* was filmed on the French Riviera, where Grace Kelly's character finds true love with a suspected cat burglar played by Cary Grant. She will actually find her prince charming during the shooting of this film, when she and Prince Rainier of Monaco are introduced by *Paris Match* reporter Pierre Galante.

WAGES OF FEAR
Henri-Georges Clouzot
1951
Yves Montand, Charles Vanel
Two actors eat lunch in front of the actual barracks that served as a concentration camp for "nomads" in France's Camargue region during World War II. Hundreds of gypsies were rounded up and detained here between 1942 and 1944. Clouzot transformed these barracks into a Mexican village for the purposes of his film, but the sinister place will be destroyed after shooting.

STROMBOLI
Roberto Rossellini
1949
**Ingrid Bergman,
Roberto
Rossellini**
As soon as they
saw each other,
Bergman and
Rossellini fell in
love. But because
they were both
married, their
liaison shocked
America, and
the neo-realist
film they made
together was
boycotted in
the U.S.
It was finally
released in a
version re-edited
by Alfred Werker.
Ingrid Bergman
would be
shunned in
Hollywood until
1956, after she
had left Rossellini.

**THE PROUD
ONES**
Yves Allégret
1953
Gérard Philipe
Despite the
scorching heat,
the boyishly
handsome Gérard
Philipe falls in
love with Mexico.
On his days off,
he rents a small
plane to explore
the country with
his wife, Anne.

**BONJOUR
TRISTESSE**
Otto Preminger
1957
**Jean Seberg,
Mylène
Demongeot,
Otto Preminger,
Deborah Kerr,
David Niven**
"One thing I'm
sure about,"
Preminger said,
"is that as long as
there are women,
there will be
material for a
good script."
Jean Seberg,
the nineteen-
year-old actress
he had debuted
the preceding
year in
Saint Joan,
is enchanted
by both Paris
and the Riviera
during filming.
She will settle
permanently
in France after
starring in Jean-
Luc Godard's
1959 movie
Breathless.
(Photo: C.
Azoulay)

THE OTHER SIDE OF THE WIND
Orson Welles
1971
Orson Welles
Facing the Nevada desert at lunchtime, Welles is perhaps dreaming up the next scenes for a film that is destined to remain a mirage. He wrote the script with Oja Kodar, his last companion in life, and chose John Huston as his leading man. This eccentric Franco-Iranian co-production was shot sporadically between 1970 and 1974 in the U.S. and in Europe. Apart from Huston, other directors will make appearances as actors: Peter Bogdanovich, Norman Foster, Curtis Harrington, Henry Jaglom, Paul Mazursky, Dennis Hopper and Claude Chabrol. The producers eventually abandoned the film—ironically, a film that tells the story of an unfinished film.

THE ROOM UPSTAIRS
Georges Lacombe
1946
Jean Gabin, Marlene Dietrich
In order to follow her new lover, Jean Gabin, to France, Marlene Dietrich—"La Grande" as Gabin called her—broke off romances with both John Wayne and novelist Erich Maria Remarque. Marcel Carné originally wanted to use this ravishing couple for *Gates of the Night*, but finally decided upon Yves Montand and Nathalie Nattier instead, leaving Dietrich and Gabin free to make this film together. A complete flop, the film was released in a cut version titled *The Room Upstairs* in the U.S. The romance will not last long, but Marlene will always keep Gabin's love letters, cherishing them for life.

LET'S MAKE LOVE
George Cukor
1960
Yves Montand, Simone Signoret, Marilyn Monroe, Arthur Miller
After Yves Montand's singing triumph on Broadway, Marilyn Monroe insists on having him as her costar in this movie. During the film's early stages, the French heartthrob and his wife, Simone Signoret, stay at the Beverly Hills Hotel in a bungalow next door to the one occupied by Marilyn Monroe and her husband, Arthur Miller. The two couples soon become friends. An actor's strike delays production and Miller must leave for Ireland to finish up the script for *The Misfits*. At the same time, Signoret is due in Italy to star in Antoni Pietrangeli's *Adua and Her Friends*…

LET'S MAKE LOVE
George Cukor
1960
**Marilyn Monroe,
Yves Montand**
Simone Signoret's
"premonitions"
about the title
of the movie
prove accurate.
As soon as
Monroe and
Montand are
alone they fall into
each other's
arms. This liaison
will last the entire
two months it
takes to finish
the film, and
will quickly
become hot
gossip around
town. Monroe
becomes
distraught upon
hearing Montand
minimize the
importance of
their love story
in an interview
he does while
playing in Tony
Richardson's
Sanctuary.

BECKET
Peter Glenville
1963
**Elizabeth Taylor,
Richard Burton**
In this scene, Liz Taylor is just an onlooker. This American film was shot in England, and was made by a team of solely British actors and technicians. Taylor and Burton had already worked together—in *Cleopatra* and *The V.I.P.s*, where they embarked upon their famous romance—and both are seeking divorces from previous spouses. They would not appear together in a film (Vincente Minnelli's *The Sandpiper*) until after their marriage on March 15, 1964.

LA STRADA
Federico Fellini
1953
**Federico Fellini,
Giulietta Masina**
They married in 1943, and Giulietta Masina became Fellini's "guardian angel" according to friend Alberto Sordi. Initially a radio actress, she began her film career in movies written by Fellini (Rossellini's *Paisà* and Lattuada's *Senza Pietà*) before appearing in films actually directed by him. First prize at the 1954 Venice Film Festival will be their first shared triumph.

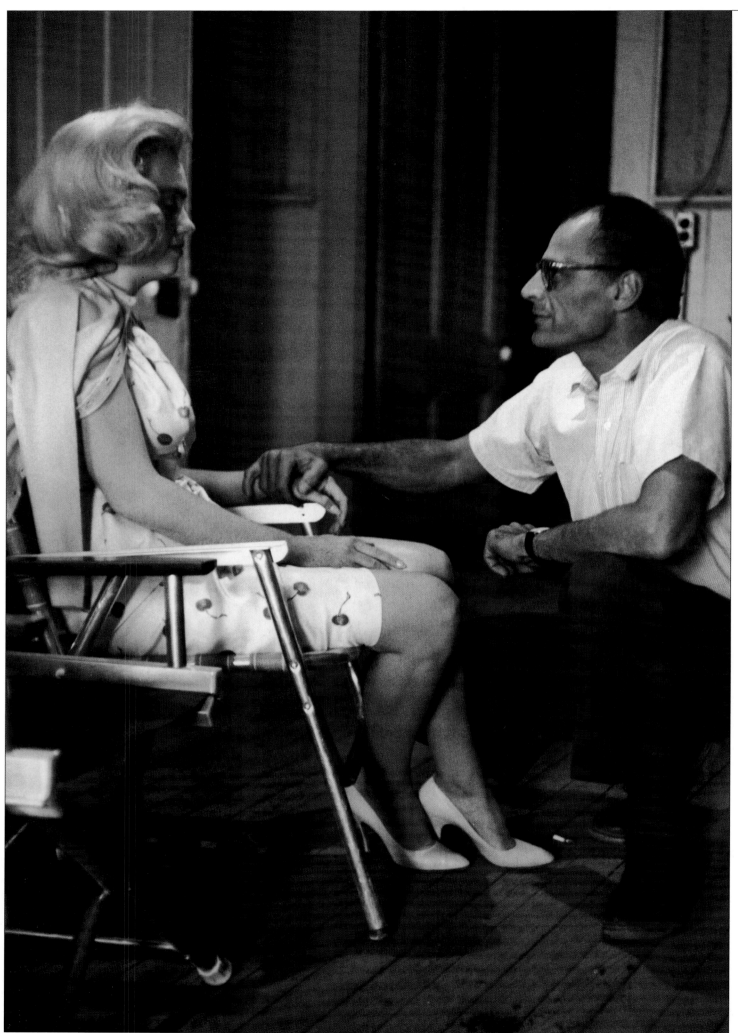

THE MISFITS
John Huston
1960
Marilyn Monroe, Arthur Miller
After four years of marriage, something is irreparably damaged between the writer and the star—Miller cannot forgive Marilyn for her affair with Yves Montand. During the shooting in Reno, they won't share the same hotel room. Less than a year later, and as soon as their divorce is announced, Miller will become engaged to a photographer he met while working on *The Misfits*.

THE LADY FROM SHANGHAI
Orson Welles
1946
Orson Welles, Rita Hayworth
Before filming began, Welles called the press to make a public spectacle of cutting Rita Hayworth's famous long tresses. He had already convinced her to dye her hair blonde. This will be their farewell movie; the magnitude of the film's failure will hasten the demise of their already ailing thirteen-year marriage.

**AND GOD...
CREATED
WOMAN**
Roger Vadim
**1956
Roger Vadim,
Brigitte Bardot,
Christian
Marquand
(at the window)**
Bardot plays
Juliette, the
incarnation
of immorality,
aptly named after
the infamous
Marquis de Sade
character.
Thanks to this
film, Vadim's first,
his young wife
will become
a universal
sex symbol.
Vadim wrote
in his memoir,
*Memories of the
Devil*: "This film
would set in
motion the
legend-making
machine."

LOVE WITH THE PROPER STRANGER
Robert Mulligan
1963
Steve McQueen, Natalie Wood
The love story unfolding on camera continues off screen. Natalie Wood is a single woman after divorcing Robert Wagner the year before (she will marry him again in 1972), but Steve McQueen is still married to Neile Adams. As a result, the romance will have no future.

LIZA
Marco Ferreri
1971
Marcello Mastroianni, Catherine Deneuve
Deneuve plays a wealthy and elegant woman who will go to any lengths to capture the heart of a cynical loner played by Mastroianni. In real life, filming this movie together on the isle of Carvallo in Corsica is the couple's honeymoon. The following year, their daughter, Chiara, will be born.

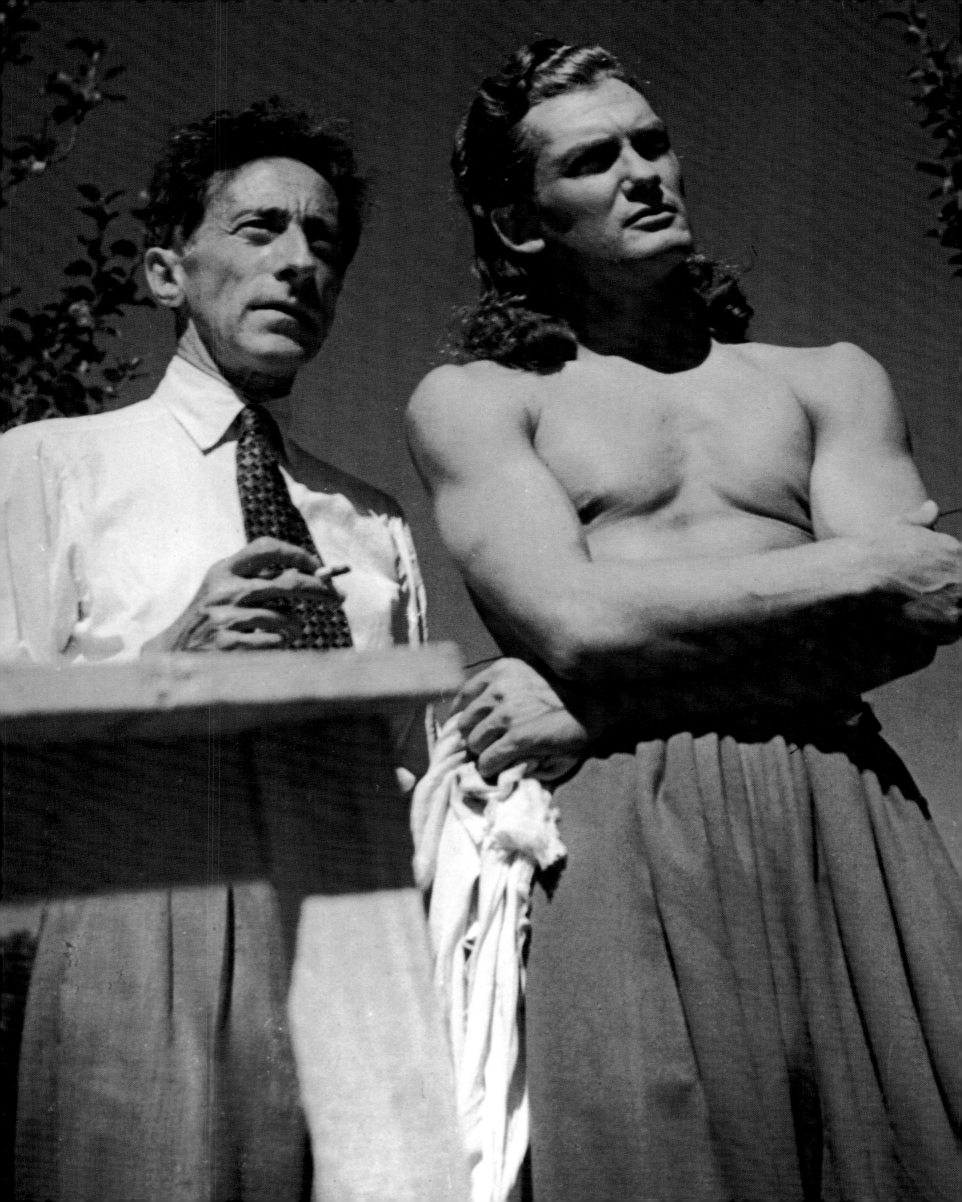

BEAUTY AND THE BEAST
Jean Cocteau
1945
Jean Cocteau, Jean Marais

"Everyone adored Cocteau. I knew right away that he was to be the love of my life," said Jean Marais. Of the three characters he played for Cocteau, the ember-eyed monster in *Beauty and the Beast* was his favorite. Cocteau wanted Beauty to fall in love with the Beast without having to transform him into Prince Charming, but the producers imposed the more conventional ending.

MUTINY ON THE BOUNTY
Lewis Milestone
1961
Marlon Brando, Tarita

At the tender age of eighteen, Marlon Brando's first wife, Movita, played opposite Clark Gable in Frank Lloyd's 1935 version of this film. Tarita, the young Polynesian woman who plays opposite Brando in the remake, will completely beguile Brando (who takes Gable's role), becoming his third wife in 1962. Movita was seven years older than Brando, Tarita seventeen years his junior.

LETTERS FROM MY WINDMILL
Marcel Pagnol
1954
Marcel Pagnol, his wife **Jacqueline** and their son **Frédéric**

This is Pagnol's final film, although he will direct a made-for-TV movie in 1967 entitled *Le Curé de Cucugnan*. Jacqueline, Pagnol's wife since 1945, starred in several of his films, including *La Belle Meunière* (1948) and *Manon of the Spring* (1952). But she won't act in this one. Their son Frédéric (pictured here) was born in 1948.

THE TRIAL
Orson Welles
1962
Orson Welles and his daughter Beatrice
Born in 1955, from his marriage to Italian actress Paola Mori, Beatrice is Welles's third daughter, after Christopher, born in 1937 of his union with Virginia Nicholson, and Rebecca, born in 1944 from his marriage to Rita Hayworth. Beatrice will play a small part in *Chimes at Midnight*.

RIO BRAVO
Howard Hawks
1958
John Wayne and his son John Ethan
"The Duke" was fascinated by Ethan Edwards, whom he portrayed in John Ford's 1955 film *The Searchers*. When Wayne's sixth child is born that same year, he will honor Edwards by naming his son after him—adding Ethan to his own first name. John Ethan will play alongside his father in Howard Hawks's *Rio Lobo* and George Sherman's *Big Jake*.

**A COUNTESS
FROM HONG
KONG**
Charlie Chaplin
1966
Charlie Chaplin,
his wife **Oona,**
his daughter
Annette
and his son
Christopher
It's a happy day
when Chaplin's
wife, Oona,
visits him on the
set, accompanied
by the youngest
of their eight
children, Annette
(b.1959) and
Christopher
(b.1962).
His three eldest
daughters, Geraldine
(b.1944),
Josephine
(b. 1949) and
Victoria (b.1951),
play small roles
in the movie.
Sydney (b.1927),
Chaplin's son
from his earlier
marriage to Lita
Grey, also has a
part in the film.

THE LIST OF ADRIAN MESSENGER
John Huston
1962
John Huston and his son Tony
Tony (b.1950), who plays in the film under the name of Walter Anthony Huston, is the eldest of Huston's three children. Huston will later adopt two more kids.

GUNS FOR SAN SEBASTIAN
Henri Verneuil
1967
Anthony Quinn and his sons Francesco and Daniele
Back in his native Mexico for Verneuil's film, Anthony Quinn, who has just remarried, is a prolific father—the two children pictured here, Francesco (b.1963) and Daniele (b.1964), were preceded by five other children and followed by a brother who is already a year old. Between 1972 and 1996, the actor will father four more sons and a daughter.

RETURN OF THE SEVEN
Burt Kennedy
1966
Yul Brynner and his daughter Victoria
A new team of actors flanks Yul Brynner, the only original cast member from John Sturges's *Magnificent Seven*. During filming in Spain, he gets to spend a lot of time with Victoria, his only daughter (b.1962).

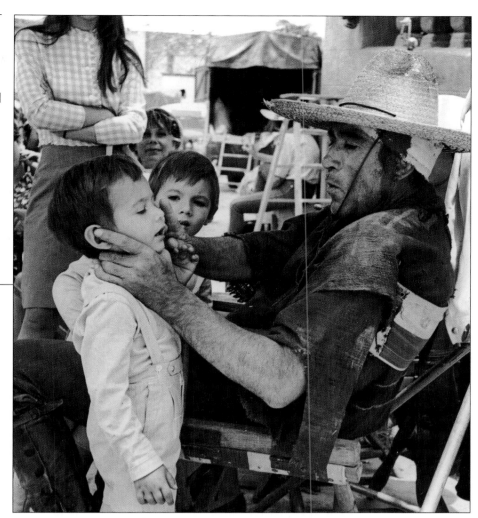

KIM
Victor Saville
1950
**Errol Flynn,
his daughters
Deirdre and Rory
and his son Sean**
Flynn poses here
with daughters
Deirdre (b.1945)
and Rory (b.1947)
from his union
with Nora
Eddington, and his
son Sean (b.1941)
from his union
with Lili Damita.
Sean began his
acting career in
Tulio Demicheli's
1961 film *The Son
of Captain Blood*,
but becomes a
photojournalist in
1967. He would
work all over the
world for many
publications.
In 1970, he
disappears in
Cambodia,
probably killed
by the Khmer
Rouge.

LUDWIG
Luchino Visconti
1972
**Romy Schneider
and her son David**
Romy Schneider's
only son, David,
was born in 1966,
shortly after her
marriage to Harry
Meyen, her costar
in Terence Young's
film *Triple Cross*.
David will die
tragically on
July 5, 1981
while trying to
scale a high fence.
Overcome with
grief, Schneider
will follow him less
than a year later.

A MATTER OF RESISTANCE
Jean-Paul Rappeneau
1965
Catherine Deneuve and her son **Christian**
Christian Vadim, son of Catherine Deneuve and Roger Vadim, was born June 18, 1963. He will make his acting debut in his father's 1982 *Surprise Party.*

ZORRO
Duccio Tessari
1974
Alain Delon and his son **Anthony**
"I became Zorro to please my son," declares Delon. Born in 1964, Anthony will become an actor, playing in films by Alberto Lattuada, Francesco Rosi, José Pinheiro and Thomas Gilou.

ANNE OF THE THOUSAND DAYS
Charles Jarrott
1969
Elizabeth Taylor
Encumbered by her sixteenth-century costume, Liz Taylor's golf game suffers. To be near Richard Burton, who stars in this film, she agrees to make a short appearance as an extra. Since the multimillionaire superstar was paid $35 for her effort, one must assume she did it for fun.

**THE BELOVED/
THE RESTLESS**
*George Pan
Cosmatos*
1970
Raquel Welch
Although he would later direct *Rambo: First Blood Part II*, Cosmatos's first film is a low-budget melodrama shot on a Greek island. Raquel Welch seems to be having a good time with the locals, but the producers at Metro Goldwyn Mayer did not find it worthy of release. It finally came out in 1981 under a new name— *The Restless*—thanks to a small distribution company that rescued it from obscurity.

THE WAY WE WERE
Sydney Pollack
1973
In the forefront:
Robert Redford, Barbra Streisand

Part of this film is set in late-1930's Hollywood. This tribute to the Marx Brothers—where Streisand impersonates Harpo and Redford wears Groucho's signature look—was inspired by an actual birthday party thrown for Groucho Marx, where all of the guests dressed up as Groucho, but Groucho himself came as Harpo.

THE BUSTER KEATON STORY
Sidney Sheldon
1956
Donald O'Connor, Buster Keaton

"It was both a wonderful and a strange experience to work with Donald O'Connor," Buster Keaton recalls enigmatically in his memoirs. The "King of Slapstick" sold the rights to his life story to Paramount for $50,000. Hired to work with O'Connor and show the actor his old gags, Keaton quickly became disillusioned with the movie. The script took such liberties with the facts of the silent star's life that Natalie Talmadge, Keaton's first wife, sued Paramount for $5 million in damages.

THE BLOCKHOUSE
Clive Rees
1973
Per Oscarsson, Peter Sellers, Charles Aznavour
The Blockhouse is one of those rare films where not a single woman appears. In spite of the impression given by this photograph, this is not a comedy, but rather a claustrophobic drama where Per Oscarsson, Peter Sellers and Charles Aznavour are trapped in a suffocating underground bunker in Normandy on D-Day.

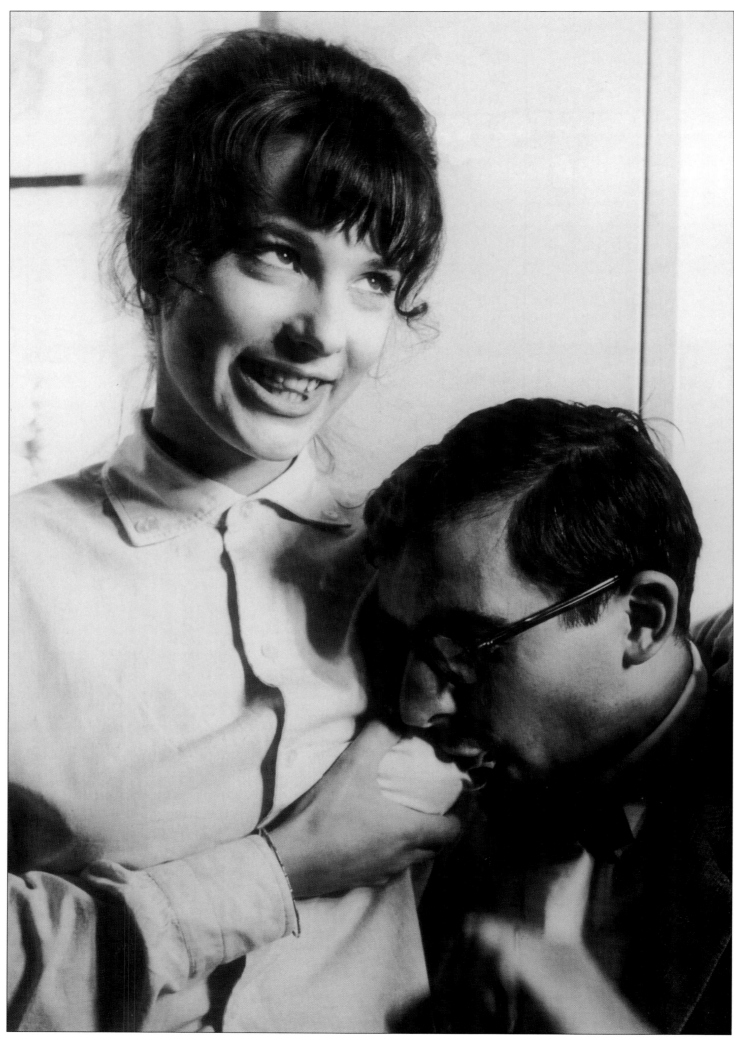

WISE GUYS
Claude Chabrol
1959
Bernadette Lafont, Claude Chabrol
Bernadette Lafont is a star of the French New Wave movement and Claude Chabrol is one of its most influential directors.
This will be the fourth time in two years that they have worked together. "Claude," Bernadette later wrote, "is a show unto himself, but he is twofold. One hour of conversation with him is enough to see his split personality."

CONTEMPT
Jean-Luc Godard
1963
Brigitte Bardot, Jean-Luc Godard
Jean-Luc Godard wanted to cast Kim Novak for the lead role, but coproducer Carlo Ponti was pulling for Sophia Loren, the love of his life. Brigitte Bardot was ultimately hired. "Thanks to her," Godard said, "everything was easy and everyone was happy." Oddly enough, the sex symbol and the avant-garde director got along very well. One day when Bardot was moody and uncooperative, Godard started walking on his hands. She laughed at this, and from that day on, she would comply with his every wish.

ONE-EYED JACKS
Marlon Brando
1959
Marlon Brando

Marlon Brando, who produced this western, initially wanted Stanley Kubrick to direct, before capriciously deciding to direct it himself. After six months of preparation, the shooting took another six months and produced nearly 200 miles of footage—the budget jumped from $1.8 to $6 million. Paramount was furious, and cut the original length of the film (nearly five hours) by half. After a year of negotiation, Brando would agree to shoot a new ending where the heroine (Pina Pellicer) survives in the end. He will never attempt to direct another movie.

A COUNTESS FROM HONG KONG
Charlie Chaplin
1966
Charlie Chaplin, Sophia Loren, Geraldine Chaplin (in background)
April 16, 1966: In London on the set of his last movie, Chaplin celebrates his 70th birthday. As he is about to slice the cake, he characteristically provides a humorous charade—not able to bear piercing his marzipan effigy, he instead turns the knife upon himself. The "little man" and his masterpieces will never die. The eight-year-old girl amused by this comic scene is the daughter of Tippi Hedren, Melanie Griffith. She will make her acting debut in 1969.

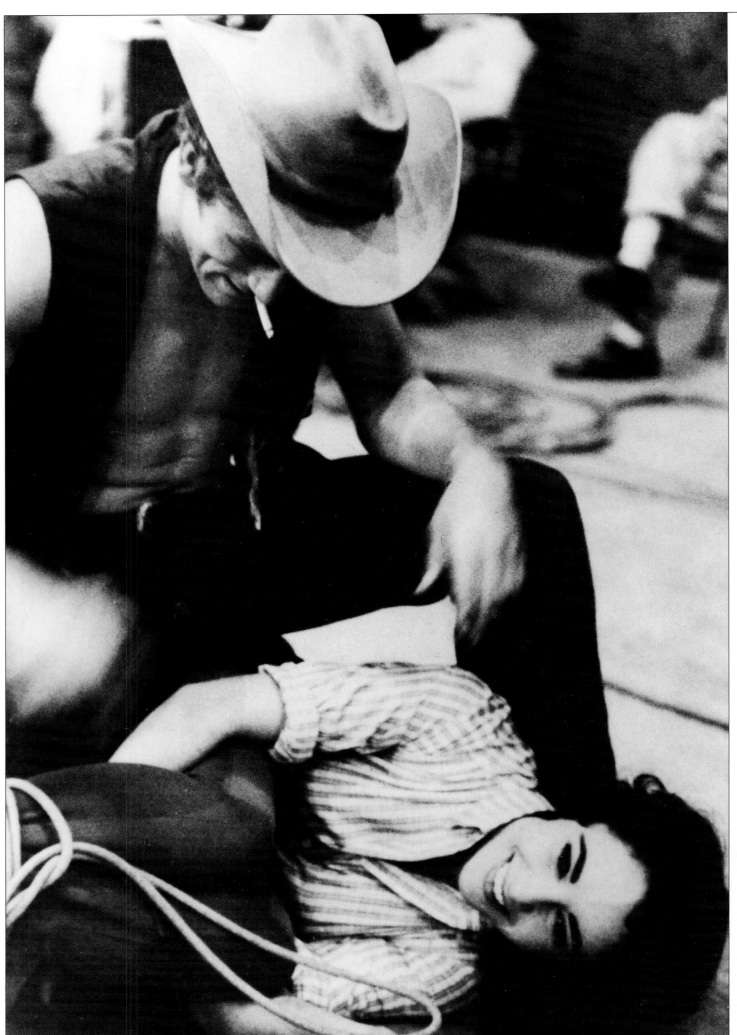

GIANT
George Stevens
1955
James Dean, Elizabeth Taylor
James Dean developed a severe crush on Liz Taylor when they met shooting *Giant*. Throughout filming, he will do anything to win her. Shortly after the film wraps, Dean will die in an automobile accident on September 30, 1955. Taylor is so distraught by this tragedy that she is hospitalized for two weeks.

LAWRENCE OF ARABIA
David Lean
1961
Peter O'Toole
Peter O'Toole keeps his sense of humor in spite of the desert's scorching sun and his newfound fame—he has been chosen over none other than Marlon Brando, Montgomery Cliff, Dirk Bogarde, Richard Burton, Anthony Perkins and Albert Finney to play the intrepid Lawrence. Alain Delon, Horst Buchholtz, Christian Marquand and Maurice Ronet competed for the Sheik Ali part, which was finally given to Omar Sharif.

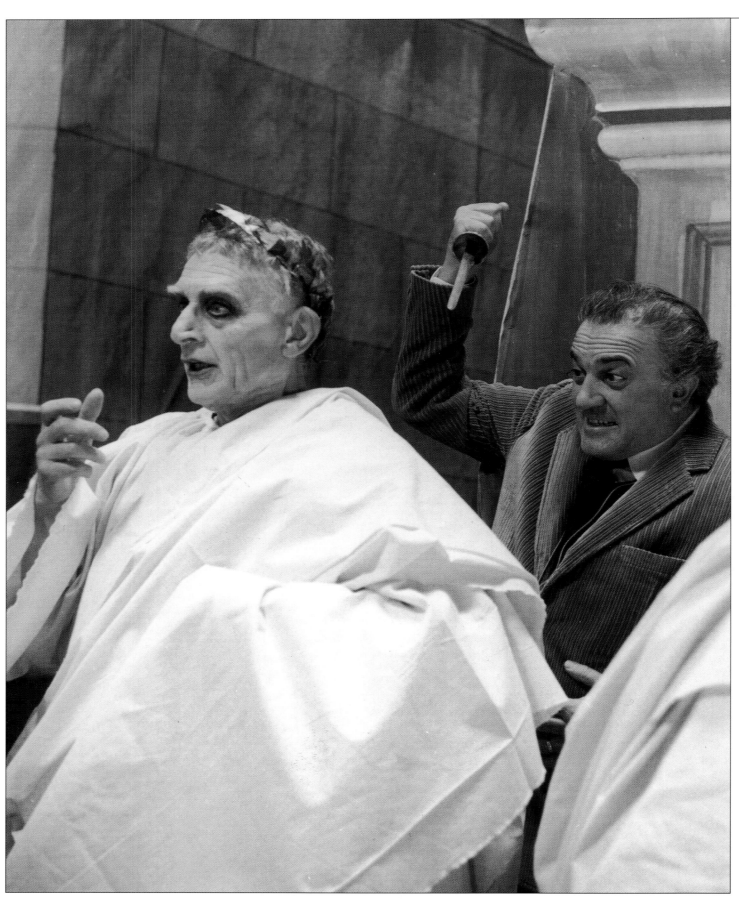

FELLINI'S ROMA
Federico Fellini
1971
Federico Fellini
"My life story is quite a banal one," Fellini said toward the end of his life. "I did exactly what I wanted by continuing to play with marionettes just like when I was a kid: I dressed them up, put makeup on them and brought them into the limelight. Luckily, I got paid to do it."

DAUGHTERS OF DESTINY
Christian-Jaque
1953
Martine Carol, Paolo Stoppa
The actors don't seem to take themselves too seriously in this film about three legendary women— Elizabeth I, Lysistrata and Joan of Arc. Carried away by an atmosphere of camaraderie and high spirits off the set, Martine Carol and Paolo Stoppa make funny faces but can't stop themselves once the cameras are rolling.

ORPHEUS
Jean Cocteau
1949
**Jean Cocteau,
Juliette Gréco**
Juliette Gréco's long hair makes Jean Cocteau the perfect goatee. A singer and an actress, Gréco fascinates the Paris literati—Jean-Paul Sartre, Raymond Queneau and François Mauriac all write lyrics for her songs. Following her acting debut with Cocteau, Darryl F. Zanuck would attempt to turn her into a Hollywood star.

THE PLEDGE
Sean Penn
2001
Jack Nicholson
Ever the joker, Jack Nicholson will go to any lengths to entertain the film crew. Even after roles under directors of such stature as Roger Corman, he was never more than a costar until finally attaining stardom in Dennis Hopper's 1969 *Easy Rider.* Despite the rumors, Jack is not related to James H. Nicholson, the legendary head of American International Pictures, in whose films he often appeared.

IN HARM'S WAY
Otto Preminger
1964
**John Wayne,
Kirk Douglas**
"Everything
separated us,"
Douglas said of
John Wayne,
"starting with
our political
differences.
But in spite of
this, he wanted
to get me in a
movie with him
for years.
Our relations
were always
cordial. Of course
we didn't see
much of each
other after the
film: we might
have met for
dinner once.
We didn't really
have much to say
to each other...."

A COUNTESS FROM HONG KONG
Charlie Chaplin
1966
Marlon Brando, Charlie Chaplin
Moments of complicity are rare between these two very different men. For Brando, Chaplin is "a kind old gentleman" with obsolete methods, whose orders he executes without discussion. "We do just as he says. He shows us how, because he has no idea what a scene will be like until he acts it himself." Brando speaks of his leading lady less equivocally. "If I die," he asserts, "there won't be a picture of Sophia Loren crying on my grave."

THE TRUTH
Henri-Georges Clouzot,
1960
Henri-Georges Clouzot, Brigitte Bardot
Although her relationship with director Henri-Georges Clouzot was a stormy one, this turned out to be the role Bardot was most proud of. To make the suicide scene more real, he tried to keep Bardot in such a depressed state that once filming is over, she will actually attempt to take her own life.

GAS-OIL
Gilles Grangier
1955
Jeanne Moreau, Jean Gabin
It's Jean Gabin's first time working with Michel Audiard who will become his favorite screenwriter. But Gabin's films are always liberally sprinkled with his own signature patois for which he became famous. For example, to express his fondness and admiration for Jeanne Moreau, Gabin refers to her as "a BSA first-class cycling track." This seemingly obscure endearment refers to a famous cycling track in Paris, which, back in the 1920s, was plastered with billboards promoting a brand of ball-bearings. In cycling argot, this brand stood for excellence and superior quality—a compliment of the highest order!

CLEOPATRA
Joseph L. Mankiewicz
1962
Roddy McDowall (left), **Richard Burton** (right)
Richard Burton exhibits rare lightheartedness on the set of this blockbuster production beset by difficulties. Conceived in 1958, the shooting started in London in 1960 under the direction of Rouben Mamoulian. Filming had to be interrupted several times due to bad weather and Liz Taylor's lengthy illness. Things will pick up again in Cinecittà, Italy in September 1961, with new director Joseph L. Mankiewicz. Twentieth Century Fox will reach the verge of bankruptcy, however, as further difficulties cause filming to last well over a year.

THE RETURN OF DON CAMILLO
Julien Duvivier
1952
Fernandel
Could this be Count Dracula? No, it's Don Camillo, the loony priest! Just one year after Duvivier directed *The Little World of Don Camillo*, Fernandel gets to wear his priest's robe once again. Duvivier wanted the character to die at the end of the movie: "Or else, I'll be forced one day to make *The Son of Don Camillo* or *Don Camillo Meets Frankenstein*." The producers were very much against this, and Fernandel was to revive the role once again in Carmine Gallone's 1955 *Don Camillo's Big Fight*.

THE BRIDGE ON THE RIVER KWAI
David Lean
1956
Unknown actress, William Holden
Bathing in the jungle can be fun! The storyline for this film takes place in Burma, but because a civil war is raging there, filming must be done in Ceylon (the future Sri Lanka). *The Bridge on the River Kwai* will receive seven Oscars and gross $30 million, covering production costs ten times over.

THE TRIAL
Orson Welles
1962
Orson Welles, Anthony Perkins
The director and leading actor take a jovial break in Paris on the banks of the Seine. The filming of *The Trial* started in a studio near Paris, continued in Zagreb and Rome, and finally concluded back in Paris in the old Orsay train station, which was then being threatened with demolition.

JULES AND JIM
François Truffaut
1961
François Truffaut, Jeanne Moreau
In a 1967 letter to his favorite director, Alfred Hitchcock, Truffaut wrote: "Jeanne Moreau is the ideal actress to work with. She is optimistic about everything, is completely dedicated to the film she's working on, has a quick mind, and is always in a good mood....
On the set she is ready to act fast or slow, be happy or sad, serious or funny and will comply with the director's every wish.
If a crisis occurs, you can rely on her for help and support."

PRÊT-À-PORTER
Robert Altman
1994
Marcello Mastroianni, Sophia Loren
Nothing but elegance and superstardom on the set of *Prêt-à-Porter*. This satirical "documentary" on the world of fashion features legendary movie stars, as well as top fashion luminaries. Designers Claude Montana, Thierry Mugler, Sonia Rykiel, Jean Paul Gaultier, Christian Lacroix, Issey Miyake and Gianfranco Ferré, and top models Christy Turlington, Helena Christensen, Naomi Campbell, Claudia Schiffer and Linda Evangelista all appear as themselves.

D.: director — Pr.: production — Sc.: script — Dial.: dialog — Ph.: photography — Comp.: music composer — Set: set design — Chor.: choreography — Ma.: makeup — Sp. eff.: special effects — Tech. cons.: technical consultant — Art. cons.: artistic consultant — Sup.: supervision — Ass.: assistant director.
The year indicated is the year of filming.

AFRICAN QUEEN, THE. USA/UK, 1951. D.: John Huston. Sc.: James Agee, John Huston, based on a novel by C.S. Forester. Ph.: Jack Cardiff. Ass.: Guy Hamilton. Pr.: United Artists (Hollywood), Horizon Pictures, Romulus (London). With Humphrey Bogart, Katharine Hepburn, Robert Morley, Peter Bull. 153

AND GOD... CREATED WOMAN (*Et Dieu... créa la femme*). France, 1956. D.: Roger Vadim. Pr.: Raoul J. Lévy. With Brigitte Bardot, Curd Jürgens, Jean-Louis Trintignant, Christian Marquand, Georges Poujouly, Isabelle Corey, Jane Marken. 186–187

ANNE OF THE THOUSAND DAYS. USA, 1969. D.: Charles Jarrott. Based on a play by Maxwell Anderson. Pr.: Universal. With Geneviève Bujold, Richard Burton, Irène Papas, Anthony Quayle. 206–207

ANTONY AND CLEOPATRA (*Marco Antonio y Cleopatra / Antonius und Cleopatra*). UK/Spain/Switzerland, 1972. D.: Charlton Heston. 2nd team: Joe Canutt. Based on a story by William Shakespeare. Ass.: Fraser C. Heston. Pr.: Rank, Folio Film Ltd. (London), Izaro Film (Madrid), Transac (Zurich). With Charlton Heston, Hildegarde Neil, Eric Porter, John Castle, Fernando Rey, Carmen Sevilla, Freddie Jones, Fernando Bilbao, Luis Barboo. 103

APOCALYPSE NOW. USA, 1977–79. D.: Francis Ford Coppola. Based on *Heart of Darkness* by Joseph Conrad. Prod.: Omni Zoetrope, for United Artists. With Martin Sheen, Robert Duvall, Marlon Brando, Dennis Hopper, Harrison Ford, Frederic Forrest. 104

AROUND THE WORLD IN EIGHTY DAYS. USA; 1955. D.: Michael Anderson [and Sidney Smith (not credited)]. Based on a novel by Jules Verne. Pr.: Michael Todd, William Cameron Menzies, for United Artists. With David Niven, Cantinflas [Mario Moreno], Shirley MacLaine, Robert Newton, Buster Keaton, John Gielgud, Marlene Dietrich, Cedric Hardwicke, Peter Lorre, George Raft, John Carradine, Frank Sinatra. 32–33

AUSTERLITZ (*Napoleone ad Austerlitz / Austerlic*). France/Italy/Yugoslavia/Liechtenstein, 1960. D.: Abel Gance, with the collaboration of Roger Richebé and Nelly Kaplan. Ph.: Henri Alekan. Pr.: Lyra Film (Paris), Galatea (Milan), Dubrava Film (Zagreb), Michael Arthur Films (Vaduz). With Pierre Mondy, Martine Carol, Claudia Cardinale, Vittorio De Sica, Jack Palance, Michel Simon, Orson Welles, Jean-Louis Trintignant. 138–139

BALL OF FIRE. USA, 1941. D.: Howard Hawks. Sc.: Billy Wilder, Thomas Monroe, Charles Brackett. Pr.: Samuel Goldwyn, for United Artists. With Gary Cooper, Barbara Stanwyck, Oscar Homolka, Dana Andrews. 15

BARABBAS. Italy, 1962. D.: Richard Fleischer. Based on a novel by Pär Lagerkvist. Pr.: Dino De Laurentiis, for Columbia. With Anthony Quinn, Vittorio Gassman, Jack Palance, Silvana Mangano, Michael Gwynn, Ernest Borgnine. 136–137

BARBARELLA. France/Italy, 1967. D.: Roger Vadim. Based on a comic book by Jean-Claude Forest. Art. cons.: Jean-Claude Forest. Pr.: Marianne Productions (Paris), Dino de Laurentiis (Rome). With Jane Fonda, John Phillip Law, Anita Pallenberg, Ugo Tognazzi, David Hemmings, Marcel Marceau, Claude Dauphin. 84

BAREFOOT CONTESSA, THE. USA, 1953–54. D.: Joseph L. Mankiewicz. Pr.: Figaro Incorporated. With Humphrey Bogart, Ava Gardner, Edmond O'Brien, Marius Goring, Valentina Cortese, Bessie Love. 54

BEAUTIES OF THE NIGHT (*Les Belles de nuit*). France/Italy, 1952. D.: René Clair. Comp.: Georges Van Parys. Set: Léon Barsacq. Ass.: Michel Boisrond. Pr.: Franco London Film (Paris), Angelo Rizzoli (Milan). With Gérard Philipe, Martine Carol, Gina Lollobrigida, Magali Vendeuil, Raymond Bussières, Paolo Stoppa, Pierre Palau. 76

BEAUTY AND THE BEAST (*La Belle et la Bête*). France, 1945–46. D.: Jean Cocteau. Based on a novel by Marie Leprince de Beaumont. Tech. cons.: René Clément. Art. cons.: Christian Bérard. Ph.: Henri Alekan. Ma.: Hagop Arakélian. Comp.: Georges Auric. Pr.: André Paulvé. With Jean Marais, Josette Day, Marcel André, Mila Parély, Michel Auclair. 192

BECKET. USA, 1963. D.: Peter Glenville. Based on a play by Jean Anouilh. Pr.: Paramount. With Richard Burton, Peter O'Toole, John Gieguld, Donald Wolfit, Martita Hunt, Pamela Brown. 182

BELOVED, THE or **THE RESTLESS**. USA/Greece, 1970. D.: George [Yorgo] Pan Cosmatos. Pr.: Metro Goldwyn Mayer (Hollywood), Curtwel (Athens). With Raquel Welch, Richard Johnson, Jack Hawkins, Flora Robson, Renato Romano, Françoise Pascal. 208–209

BIRDS, THE. USA, 1963. D.: Alfred Hitchcock. Sc.: Evan Hunter, based on a novel by Daphne Du Maurier. Comp.: Bernard Herrmann, Oskar Sala. Pr.: Universal. With Tippi Hedren, Rod Taylor, Jessica Tandy, Suzanne Pleshette. 112–113

BLOCKHOUSE, THE. UK, 1973. D.: Clive Rees. Based on *Le Blockhaus* byJean-Paul Clébert. Pr.: Audley Associates, Galacticus, Hemdale. With Peter Sellers, Charles Aznavour, Per Oscarsson, Jeremy Kemp, Peter Vaughan. 212–213

BLUE MAX, THE. UK/USA, 1965. D.: John Guillermin. 2nd team: Anthony Squire. Based on a novel by Jack D. Hunter. Comp.: Jerry Goldsmith. Pr.: Christian Ferry, for 20th Century Fox. With George Peppard, James Mason, Ursula Andress, Anton Diffring. 52–53, 77

BONJOUR TRISTESSE. USA, 1957. D.: Otto Preminger. Based on a novel by Françoise Sagan. Comp.: Georges Auric. Pr.: Wheel Productions, for Columbia. With Deborah Kerr, David Niven, Jean Seberg, Mylène Demongeot, Martita Hunt, Juliette Gréco. 172–173

BONNIE AND CLYDE. USA, 1967. D.: Arthur Penn. Pr.: Tatira-Hiller Productions, Warren Beatty, for Warner Bros./Seven Arts. With Warren Beatty, Faye Dunaway, Michael J. Pollard, Gene Hackman, Estelle Parsons. 23

BOOM! UK, 1968. D.: Joseph Losey. Sc.: Tennessee Williams. Pr.: Rank, Moon Lake, World Film Services. With Elizabeth Taylor, Richard Burton, Noel Coward, Joanna Shimkus, Michael Dunn. 96–97

BRIDGE ON THE RIVER KWAI, THE. UK/USA, 1956. D.: David Lean. Sc.: Carl Foreman and Michael Wilson [not credited], based on a novel by Pierre Boulle. Pr.: Horizon Pictures (London), Columbia (Hollywood). With Alec Guinness, William Holden, Sessue Hayakawa, Jack Hawkins, André Morell. 236

BUSTER KEATON STORY, THE. USA, 1956. D.: Sidney Sheldon. Tech. cons.: Buster Keaton. Pr.: Forum Productions, for Paramount. With Donald O'Connor, Larry White, Ann Blyth, Rhonda Fleming, Peter Lorre, Jackie Coogan, Cecil B. DeMille. 211

BYE BYE MONKEY (*Rêve de singe / Ciao maschio*). Italy/France, 1977. D.: Marco Ferreri. Pr.: Diciotto dicembre (Rome), Action Film, Prospectacle (Paris). With Gérard Depardieu, James Coco, Marcello Mastroianni, Gail Lawrence, William Berger, Mimsy Farmer. 19

CHIMES AT MIDNIGHT (*Campanadas a media-noche*). Spain/Switzerland, 1964–65. D.: Orson Welles. 2nd team: Jesus [Jess] Franco. Based on several plays by William Shakespeare. Pr.: Internacional Films Escolano (Madrid), Alpine Productions (Basel). With Orson Welles, Keith Baxter, John Gielgud, Jeanne Moreau, Margaret Rutherford, Marina Vlady, Walter Chiari, Fernando Rey, Ingrid Pitt. 40–41, 85, 99

CHISUM. USA, 1969. D.: Andrew V. McLaglen. Pr.: Batjac [John Wayne], for Warner Bros. With John Wayne, Forrest Tucker, Christopher George, Pamela McMyler, John Agar. 58

CLEOPATRA. USA, 1960-63. D.: Joseph L. Mankiewicz [and Rouben Mamoulian (not credited)]. 2nd team: Ray Kellog, Andrew Marton. Comp.: Alex North. Chor.: Hermes Pan. Pr.: 20th Century Fox. With Elizabeth Taylor, Richard Burton, Rex Harrison, Martin Landau, Roddy McDowall, Michael Gwynn, Marie Devereux. 22, 30, 114–115, 232–233

CLOAK AND DAGGER. USA, 1946. D.: Fritz Lang. Based on a novel by Corey Ford and Alastair MacBain. Comp.: Max Steiner. Pr.: United States Pictures, for Warner Bros. With Gary Cooper, Lilli Palmer, Vladimir Sokoloff, J. Edward Bromberg, Ludwig Stossel. 38

CONQUEST. USA, 1937. D.: Clarence Brown. Based on *Pani Walewska* by Waclaw Casiorowski. Ph.: Karl Freund. Pr.: Metro Goldwyn Mayer. With Greta Garbo, Charles Boyer, Reginald Owen, Maria Ouspenskaya, Vladimir Sokoloff, George Zucco. 117

CONTEMPT (*Le Mépris / Il disprezzo*). France/Italy, 1963. D.: Jean-Luc Godard. Based on a novel by Alberto Moravia. Pr.: Georges de Beauregard (Paris), Champion Films [Carlo Ponti] (Rome). With Brigitte Bardot, Michel Piccoli, Jack Palance, Fritz Lang, Giorgia Moll, Jean-Luc Godard. 215

the films

Photographic credits

Cover: Michael Childers/Corbis Sygma; front endpapers: Magnum; pages 2–3: Franco Pinna; pages 4–5: Dimitri Kasterine/Camera 5; pages 12–13: Carlyle Alpina Production/United Artists; page 14: Franco Pinna; page 15: Samuel Goldwyn Production/United Artists; pages 16–17: François Gragnon/*Paris Match*; page 18: United Artists; page 19: Diciotto dicembre (Rome), Action Film, Prospectacle (Paris); pages 20–21: Robert Lebeck/Studio X; page 22: Twentieth Century Fox; page 23: productions Tatira–Hiller Warren Beatty–Warner Bros./Seven Arts; pages 24–25: Gianfranco Sams; pages 26–27: Maurice Jarnoux/*Paris Match*; page 28: Tazio Secchiaroli; page 29: Jean-Claude Deutsch/*Paris Match*; page 30: Ken Danvers/Twentieth Century Fox; page 31: Bob Willoughby; pages 32–33: David Seymour/Magnum; pages 34–35: Dennis Stock/Magnum; pages 36–37: Michael Childers/Corbis Sygma; page 38 top: Robert Cohen/Rue des Archives; page 38 bottom: United States Pictures/Warner Bros; page 39: Jack Garofalo/*Paris Match*; pages 40–41: Nicolas Tikhomiroff/Magnum; pages 42–43: Lawrence Schiller/Corbis; pages 44–45: Estate of Paul Slade; page 46 top: Carlo Ponti Production, Dino de Laurentiis/Paramount; page 46 bottom: Fédération française des ciné-clubs; page 47: Riama Film Production (Rome), Gray Films Pathé Cinéma (Paris); pages 48–49: Dickens; page 50: Carlo Ponti Production/Metro Goldwyn Mayer; page 51: Magnum; pages 52–53: Claude Azoulay/*Paris Match*; page 54: Figaro Incorporated Production; page 55: Metro Goldwyn Mayer; pages 56–57: United Artists; page 58: Estate of Paul Slade; page 59: Stanley Kramer Production/Columbia Tristar Motion Picture Group; page 60: Estate of Paul Slade; page 61: Universal; pages 62–63: Paramount; pages 64–65: Columbia Tristar Motion Picture Group; page 66: Claude Azoulay/*Paris Match*; page 67: Jean-Claude Sauer/*Paris Match*; pages 68–69: Terry O'Neil; pages 70–71: Walter Carone/*Paris Match*; pages 72–73: Nancy Ellison/Corbis Sygma; pages 74–75: Associated Press; page 76: Walter Carone/*Paris Match*; page 77: Claude Azoulay/*Paris Match*; pages 78–79: Dennis Stock/Magnum; page 80: René Vital/*Paris Match*; page 81: Twentieth Century Fox; pages 82–83: Pierluigi/Reporters Associati; page 84: Magnum; page 85: Nicolas Tikhomiroff/Magnum; pages 88–89: Sam Levin; pages 90–91: Collection Bavouzet; page 92: Walter Carone/*Paris Match*; page 93: Angelo Novi/Fotografia Roma; pages 94–95: Giancolombo; pages 96–97: Rank, Moon Lake, World Film Services; page 98: Photo Izis; page 99: Nicolas Tikhomiroff/Magnum; pages 100–101: Walt Disney Studios; page 102: Roger Corbeau; page 103: Unapix Production; page 104: Dirk Halstaed; page 105: Gian Carlo Botti/Stills; pages 106–107: Jean Schmidt; pages 108–109: Lucas Film Ltd Production; pages 110–111: United Artists; pages 112–113: Universal; pages 114–115: Twentieth Century Fox; page 116: George Barris; page 117: Metro Goldwyn Mayer Studios; pages 118–119: Arthur Zinn; pages 120–121: Collection Philippe Bavouzet; pages 122–123: Pictorial Parade; pages 124–125: Bob Willoughby; pages 126–127: Franz Goess; pages 128–129: Mirisch Pictures Inc.; pages 130–131: Max G. Scheler; pages 132–133: Universal; pages 134–135: Twentieth Century Fox; pages 136–137: Italy News Photos; pages 138–139: Charles Courrière/*Paris Match*; page 140: Jacques de Potier/*Paris Match*; page 141: Pierluigi/Reporters Associati; page 142: Twentieth Century Fox; page 143: Claude Azoulay/*Paris Match*; page 144: Pierre Vals; page 145: Giancolombo; pages 146–147: Tazio Secchiaroli; pages 148–149: Patrice Habans/*Paris Match*; pages 150–151: Jean-Pierre Darlo; page 152: Terry O'Neil; page 153: United Artists (Hollywood), Horizon Pictures Romulus (London); pages 154–155: British Lion Production, London Films, Lopert Films (London), United Artists (Hollywood); page 156: Charles Courrière/*Paris Match*; page 157 top: Sipa; page 157 bottom: Sanchez; pages 160–161: Pierluigi/Reporters Associati; page 162: Curt Gunther; page 163: Paramount; pages 164–165: Walter Carone/*Paris Match*; pages 166–167: François Page/*Paris Match*; page 168: Edward Quinn; page 169: Pierre Vals; page 170: Daniel Filipacchi/*Paris Match*; page 171: Walter Carone/*Paris Match*; pages 172–173: Claude Azoulay/*Paris Match*; pages 174–175: Nicolas Tikhomiroff/Magnum; pages 176–177: Alcina Production; pages 178–179: Bruce Davidson/Magnum; pages 180–181: John Bryson; page 182: André Lefebvre/*Paris Match*; page 183: Angeli; page 184: Eve Arnold/Magnum; page 185: Kobal Collection; pages 186–187: Michou Simon/*Paris Match*; pages 188–189: William Claxton/Globe Photos; pages 190–191: Jean-Claude Deutsch/*Paris Match*; page 192: Serge Lido/Sipa; page 193: Metro Goldwyn Mayer; pages 194–195: Walter Carone/*Paris Match*; page 196: Paris Europa Productions (Paris), Hisa films (Munich), Finanziaria Cinematografica Italiana (Rome), Globus Dubrava (Zagreb); page 197: Bettman/Corbis; pages 198–199: Cyril Morange; page 200: C.I.P.R.A. production (Paris), Peliculas Ernesto Enriquez (Mexico), Filmes Cinematografica (Rome); page 201 top: Doc. Pelé/Stills; page 201 bottom: Cesar Lucas; page 202: Gamma; page 203: Mario Tursi; page 204: François Gragnon/*Paris Match*; page 205: Jean-Pierre Bonnotte/Gamma; pages 206–207: Pierluigi/Reporters Associati; pages 208–209: Terry O'Neil; page 210: Steve Schapiro; page 211: Bettman/Corbis; pages 212–213: Bengt Adin; pages 214: Raymond Boyer/Sunset Boulevard; page 215: Pierluigi/Reporters Associati; pages 216–217: Paramount; pages 218–219: Universal; page 220: Sandford Roth/Rapho; page 221: Columbia Tristar Motion Picture Group; page 222: Ultra Films Production (Rome); page 223: Walter Carone/*Paris Match*; page 224: Serge Lido/Sipa; page 225: Willy Rizzo; pages 226–227: Paramount; pages 228–229: Alfred Eisenstaedt/Time Life Inc.; page 230: Paul Apoteker; page 231: Rue des Archives; pages 232–233: Ken Danvers; pages 234–235: Walter Carone/*Paris Match*; page 236: Columbia Tristar Motion Picture Group; page 237: Paris Europa Productions; pages 238–239: Production S.E.D.I.F. Films du Carrosse; pages 240–241: Jean-Claude Deutsch/*Paris Match*; back endpapers: Metro Goldwyn Mayer.

All photographs listed above come from the *Paris Match* archives. Extensive research was undertaken to correctly identify copyright owners. However, any errors or omissions brought to the publisher's attention will be corrected at the printing of the second edition.

Acknowledgments

The authors wish to thank in particular Romain Clergeat
for his precious help and his never-ending support;
Jean-Jacques Naudet for his perseverance;
Alain Genestar, Florence Rossier, Dominique d'Orglandes and Gérard Ratineaud,
who opened wide the doors of the *Paris Match* archives;
and Blandine Lepage at the Cinémathèque française.
Lastly, thanks to all the photographers, whose talent
has given us the motivation to do this book.